ATAL BIHARI
VAJPAYEE

ATAL BIHARI
VAJPAYEE

A MAN FOR ALL SEASONS

KINGSHUK NAG

Published by
Rupa Publications India Pvt. Ltd 2016
7/16, Ansari Road, Daryaganj
New Delhi 110002

Sales Centres:

Allahabad Bengaluru Chennai
Hyderabad Jaipur Kathmandu
Kolkata Mumbai

Copyright © Kingshuk Nag 2016

The views and opinions expressed in this book are the author's own and the facts are as reported by him which have been verified to the extent possible, and the publishers are not in any way liable for the same.

All rights reserved.
No part of this publication may be reproduced, transmitted, or stored in a retrieval system, in any form or by any means, electronic, mechanical, photocopying, recording or otherwise, without the prior permission of the publisher.

ISBN: 978-81-291-3776-0

First impression 2016

10 9 8 7 6 5 4 3 2 1

The moral right of the author has been asserted.

Printed by Replika Press Pvt. Ltd.

This book is sold subject to the condition that it shall not, by way of trade or otherwise, be lent, resold, hired out, or otherwise circulated, without the publisher's prior consent, in any form of binding or cover other than that in which it is published.

*For Aman Ki Asha,
the cause of peace and harmony
between India and Pakistan
that Atal Bihari Vajpayee tirelessly strove for.*

Contents

Preface	ix
Introduction	1
1. The Formative Years	18
2. Getting into Politics	29
3. Leading the Jana Sangh	44
4. Love, Life and Poetry	60
5. The Man and His Style	77
6. Janata Raj and the BJP	90
7. Witness to Ayodhya	103
8. Post Ayodhya to Prime Minister	114
9. Pursuing Peace	125
10. Dealing with the Alma Mater	140
11. Revving up the Economy	154
12. Exiting Power	164
13. A Statesman Par Excellence	175

Preface

IT WAS WHEN I was completing my book on the Bharatiya Janata Party—*The Saffron Tide: The Rise of BJP*—in the first quarter of 2014, that Kapish Mehra, Managing Director of Rupa Publications India, called me, asking whether I would like to write a biography of Atal Bihari Vajpayee. I pondered a while and realized that here was a man who had straddled the Indian political scene for half a century and been Prime Minister of the country, but there was no decent biography of his in English. This is what prompted me to agree to the proposal.

Writing the biography was both easy and difficult. Easy, because there are scores of people who knew Mr Vajpayee well and many of them were ready to share their experiences with me. Yet, as I proceeded with my research on him, I got the feeling that although many people said that they knew Mr Vajpayee well, he was deeper than would seem superficially. His easygoing ways were only a veneer. He was a deeply contemplative man and had a keen idea of what India needed. Even though he was from the BJP, which the Western press describes as a Hindu party, he realized that for any government to be successful in India, it had compulsorily to hold on to the middle ground. This is how it had been for centuries.

It is this middle ground that Mr Vajpayee attempted to hold on to in his long political career, eschewing extremities of any kind. Thus, he became the evergreen hero of Indian politics, liked by almost everybody.

Vajpayee was not a unidimensional man: apart from politics, he took keen interest in music and was himself a poet. He was also fond of good food and, above all, of good company. This made the writing of the book an interesting project. Having lived in Delhi for a large part of my life—most of the time in what was part of the New Delhi parliamentary constituency—Atal Bihari Vajpayee has been a familiar figure since my childhood. I can personally testify that he always evoked positive reactions in the minds of people and was seen as an eminently likeable guy. However, I regret that it was not possible to meet him for this book, owing to his ill health.

Apart from Kapish Mehra, I would like to thank the Publishing Director of Rupa, Ritu Vajpeyi-Mohan, for taking me through the project with ease. I am also thankful to my bosses at the *Times of India* for allowing me to undertake this project. Many people—too numerous to be named—were generous with their time and some shared deep insights. I would like to thank them all.

Kingshuk Nag

Introduction

ON THE MORNING OF 1 November 1984, Atal Bihari Vajpayee heard a commotion outside his home in New Delhi's Raisina Road. Although Atal was slightly indisposed, the decibel levels were loud enough to prompt the Bharatiya Janata Party (BJP) Member of Parliament (MP) to come out of his house. On the opposite side of the road was a taxi stand and a mob had collected there. The frenzied mob, charged by the assassination of Prime Minister Indira Gandhi the previous day by her Sikh bodyguards, wanted to avenge her killing by targeting every Sikh in sight. Most of the taxis at the stand, like at all other stands in Delhi, were driven by Sikhs. The mob wanted to burn the taxis and lynch the drivers. Alarmed by the sight, Atal hastened to the other side of the road to stop the violence. It took some time, but Atal was a familiar figure in Delhi and commanded enormous respect. The ringleaders heeded his words and the mob dispersed slowly. Atal stood at the spot till the last man had left.

Later in the day—after an emergency meeting at the BJP's headquarters at 11, Ashoka Road, where he heard harrowing tales of the targeting of Sikhs from colleagues—Atal, along with long-term associate L.K. Advani, went to see Home Minister Narasimha

Rao. The opposition leader was not satisfied with Rao's lukewarm assurance that he would look into the problem; moreover, Rao was non-committal about deploying the army on the streets as Atal suggested. Disappointed, Atal came back to the party office and told local BJP leaders like Madan Lal Khurana and Vijay Kumar Malhotra to get the party cadres in the field to protect Sikhs and their properties. Whether the diktat was really followed by the BJP cadres or whether they stood as passive spectators at many places is a matter of debate. But the fact remains that Atal rose like a leader, trying to organize his party machinery to stop the violence while the law-and-order machinery stood inert and ruling-party-inspired mobs targeted hapless Sikhs—men, women and children—and destroyed their properties.

A fortnight later, at the meeting of the national executive of the BJP, Atal openly said, 'If at some level in the ruling party this feeling had not been there that the community to which the killers [of Indira Gandhi] belonged should be taught a lesson, the disturbances would not have assumed the dimensions that they did.'

For his temerity, Atal had to pay a heavy price. He had contested his previous two elections from the New Delhi constituency and realized that he would face certain defeat from his seat in the polls that were barely two months away. In fact, to ensure that Atal lost at any cost, the Congress planned to field Amitabh Bachchan from the seat. Reading the signs, he decided to move to his hometown Gwalior, but here, too, he came a cropper and lost the elections. After all, the BJP was then just a fledgling party, only four years old, and it had managed to win just two seats across the country. (Arguably, the BJP's performance could have been better in those days of madness if its party leaders had made common cause with the Congress.) In the aftermath of his mother's assassination, Rajiv Gandhi had said, 'When a big tree falls, the earth underneath shakes,' giving courage to the marauders. Atal, on the other hand, did not make any such utterances for political gains, even though he could well have because the Sikhs, at least in those days, were not known to be part of the support base of the saffron party. As it happened, Atal's silence could well have swung some of the Hindu votes towards the Congress.

Atal did not envision the BJP as a purely Hindu party. In fact, it was at his insistence that the party chose Gandhian socialism and positive secularism as its credo at its launch on the Easter Sunday of 1980. For Atal, everything that was Bharatiya was Hindu; and in his reckoning, the term Hindu did not denote the followers of Hinduism but all those who lived in Bharat that is India. Quite early in his political life, Atal realized that India was a secular country with a tradition of tolerance for all faiths. By implication, this meant that no political party could survive and prosper in the country by espousing extreme ideologies. Thus, he wanted to fashion the BJP as a centre-of-the-road party which carried everybody along with it. In doing so, he was often at cross purposes with extreme elements of the Sangh Parivar that he was a part of.

From his early political life, leaders from across the political spectrum realized that Atal had qualities that would make him universally acceptable. Jawaharlal Nehru recognized his great potential and often promoted him by inviting and introducing him to visiting dignitaries, even though Atal was then a first-term parliamentarian. Under normal circumstances, a prime minister of the stature of Pandit Nehru would not have been expected to shower so much attention on a first-termer, especially one who came from an opposition party and did not belong to the same social background as him. In another example of Atal's universal acceptability, in the early 1970s, *Pratipaksh*, a journal of the Samyukta Socialist Party (SSP), carried an article highly critical of his role in the Quit India Movement. The writer, Arun Kumar, who was a party official, remembers how George Fernandes, widely known as a hot-headed, left-leaning trade unionist, was furious.

'Why are you trying to damage the image of this leader who is shaping up well?' Fernandes had asked Arun Kumar. (It must be noted here that this was much before Vajpayee and Fernandes came together in the Janata Party.)

Even Indira Gandhi had sought Vajpayee's opinion before sending the army to storm the Golden Temple during Operation Blue Star in June 1984. A few weeks before the operation, when Atal had gone to Bangalore for a naturopathy treatment, he had told Indira Gandhi over the phone that there must be other ways of flushing the militants out of the temple, and had warned her that the course of action she was mulling would have consequences. As later events showed, Indira Gandhi, hurtling to disaster, did not heed his advice, but she did seek his counsel nevertheless. Vajpayee, of course, admired her courage but did not agree with her politics. He compared her with Goddess Durga after the war for liberation of Bangladesh in 1971 and had no hesitation in saying so on the floor of Parliament. At the same time, he was often very harsh on Indira and sometimes even mocked her proclivity to concentrate all power in her own hands in a rhyme, often recited at public meetings in the 1980s: '*Indira Gandhi number ek, number do hai kaun? Kewal number ek, number do kaun hai; naari number ek baaki sub das numberi!*' (She is the sole decision maker in her party, she is number one, two and three...the rest are all insignificant.)

Another evidence of Atal's likeability came on 26 January 1992, when he was conferred the Padma Vibhushan by the Congress-led Narasimha Rao government that was in office at the time—an act unusual in the fact that it is not common for ruling parties to bestow this honour on opposition party representatives. In fact, Narasimha Rao also appointed Atal as the leader of the official Indian delegation to the United Nations Human Rights Commission (UNHRC) in Geneva in 1993. This was a crucial meeting because the Indian delegation had to face allegations of human rights violations in Kashmir.

Perhaps it was this ability to invoke trust that made him acceptable to the bosses of his alma mater, the Rashtriya Swayamsevak Sangh (RSS). Atal's lifestyle was far removed from that of a conservative pracharak; still, throughout the 1960s and 1970s, RSS bosses not only tolerated him but also promoted him. In fact, he was a kind of poster boy for the RSS, in spite of efforts made by political opponents to dislodge him through rumour mongering about his being hand-in-glove with top leaders of the ruling Congress party. Some rivals like Balraj Madhok espoused extreme ideologies but the RSS sarsanghchalak M.S. Golwalkar, in those heady days of the 1960s, had the practical sense to back Atal, realizing that only a man holding the middle ground could help the the political wing of the RSS (then known as the Jana Sangh) expand and consolidate. Incidentally, many analysts maintain that Golwalkar believed in extreme ideologies—some of which were clearly reflected in his writings.

More than Golwalkar's sagacity, Atal is worthy of praise for espousing a middle path in the Jana Sangh and for drawing a large part of his strength from the Arya Samaj. Although a reformist Hindu organization that believed in doing away with rituals and superstitions, Arya Samaj leaders like Swami Shraddhanand had come to grief a few decades earlier for aggressively promoting reconversions. Delhi, in the first two decades after Independence, was full of refugees who had lost their all in the partition. Many of them supported the Jana Sangh and the extreme elements harboured venomous hatred for the minorities. To carry along this support base and temper it was an extremely challenging job, but Atal did it without raising hackles. One of the first times this came to fore was in November 1966 when a group of thousands of unruly sadhus, supported by some Sangh Parivar organizations, held huge demonstrations in front of Parliament and attempted to break into the premises. Atal tried hard to calm the sadhus who were being egged on; but he was not quite successful, and there was police firing resulting in some loss of life.

In 1957, at the age of thirty-three, Atal reached Parliament for the first time. This was fairly early, considering that in those days, many old freedom fighters, some of them in their late seventies and even eighties, were ruling the roost. What brought him to the Lok Sabha were his superb oratorical skills. The then bosses of the fledgling Jana Sangh (founded in 1951), realized that Atal's way with words and the passion that he brought to his speeches were invaluable assets. Parliament helped Atal blossom, with greats like Jawaharlal Nehru and many others inspiring him. Atal's abiding interest in foreign affairs was something that was cultivated in Parliament, and his impassioned speech on Tibet in 1959 is considered by many as one of the best ever delivered on the floor of the House by any member. In his speech delivered in Hindi, Atal pointed out (and subsequent events proved that this apprehension was correct) that 'the whole aim of China is to reduce the Tibetans to a minority in their own country and destroy the Tibetan personality. It is a new phenomenon, a new type of imperialism'.

Over a period of time, Parliament was to become his second home and when Atal lost an election in 1984, he was like a fish out of water. Parliament taught him the value of democracy and democratic traditions and fashioned his political ideology. He learnt the value of cooperating with other parties on a common agenda, as well as the art of governance. Other than Nehru, Atal was greatly inspired by Jayaprakash Narayan who had come out of his retirement to launch a crusade against corruption and had united the opposition parties in their struggle against the overbearing Congress party. He was also buoyed by his experience of working as a minister in the Morarji Desai government. Although Desai had a Congress lineage, Atal realized that the former's politics was not very different from his own. Desai was old enough to be Atal's father and would admonish him at times when he felt that his minister had gone a little too far. (Atal was not alone, George Fernandes was also similarly admonished.)

The earliest political influence on Atal was of course that of the founder of the Jana Sangh, Shyama Prasad Mukherjee, who was himself a greater orator. In fact, Shyama Prasad's speech on Kashmir on the floor of Parliament had inspired Atal. It was the early demise of Shyama Prasad that pushed Atal to the forefront because the loss of the great orator, it was felt, could only be made up by Atal. Young Atal's fortunes rode on the strong support he got from the long-time party secretary, Deen Dayal Upadhyaya. From Deen Dayal, Atal learnt the value of being acceptable to all and striving for policies to do so. After the 1962 elections, Atal strove to form a common parliamentary group comprising the Jana Sangh, the Swatantra Party and the socialists. The leader of the socialists, Ram Manohar Lohia, was seen as a nationalist by the Jana Sangh. Atal's proposal came at a time when his rival leader in the party, Balraj Madhok, was pushing for a merger of the Jana Sangh and the Swatantra Party. But Atal knew that this would never materialize because the two parties had disparate support bases, so he pushed for a more feasible and practical course of action. In 1974, when the more moderate leader Jayaprakash Narayan came on the scene, Atal supported him and his movement wholeheartedly on practical considerations. Atal's point of view was that it was becoming increasingly difficult to defeat the Congress electorally because of the enormous amount of money that the party commanded.

Atal had an inborn talent for oration and forging alliances even before he joined a political party. In college, in Gwalior, Atal stood for elections for the post of secretary of the students' union and he put up his own candidate for the post of the president. This candidate was weak, and was up against a resourceful opponent. However, Atal's aggressive campaigning ensured that his candidate won.

It was the influence of his Janata government experience that made Atal insist that Gandhian socialism and positive secularism be the mottos of the newly formed BJP in 1980. However, just as it was adopting a moderate line, unlike the more uncompromisingly Hindu line of its older avatar, the Jana Sangh, the ruling Congress was becoming an increasingly Hindu party! This was during Indira Gandhi's second tenure (1980–84) when the Assam, Punjab and Kashmir problems started raising their heads. Indira's strident statements (not appreciated by the minorities), and her visible, highly publicized visits to temples and to religious gurus, evoked the vision of a Hindu leader. Thus, there was a role reversal—the Atal-led BJP adopting a moderate line and the Indira-led Congress taking a turn to the right on political issues. Atal realized that the BJP was suffering from a Jana Sangh hangover and this had to be jettisoned, whether through portrayal of the Janata Party manifesto as its own or through moderate and carefully calibrated statements.

The irony was that the RSS boss, Balasaheb Deoras, was increasingly seeing Indira's Congress as a party worth supporting at the cost of the BJP. Those in the know of things say that at the height of the Emergency in late 1976, Deoras was willing to do business with Indira. As Coomi Kapoor notes in her book on the Emergency: 'Ironically Balasaheb Deoras who was put in jail did not play such a heroic role. From prison he sent several letters to Indira Gandhi praising her leadership and these were perceived as a form of apology or a plea for pardon.' Those were bleak days and many believed that the Emergency would continue endlessly. Once Jayaprakash Narayan took the lead for the formation of the Janata Party, Deoras was enthusiastic and supported Atal's moves for merger with it. After the Janata experiment was over and the BJP under Atal embarked on a moderate course, Deoras also started energizing dormant organizations like the Vishwa Hindu Parishad (VHP) that had hitherto been controlled by sadhus and sants. Now, the VHP began to operate with the express idea of uniting Hindus. The organization was front-ended by various Hindu sants and sadhus but run with the organizational skills of RSS men. Various yatras across the length and breadth of the country and intensive yatras in cow-belt states like UP were organized for the purpose of mobilizing Hindus towards a common goal. The programmes intensified after the BJP ended up with two Lok Sabha seats in the 1984 elections that swept Rajiv Gandhi to power with 414 seats in a House of 545.

After the appalling showing in the elections, Atal was sidelined and the reins of the party were handed over to his lieutenant Lal Krishna Advani who aggressively promoted the party on a Hindu agenda for the next decade, culminating in the demolition of the Babri Masjid. Advani, a refugee from Sindh, had been an RSS worker from a young age and had been deployed to assist the Jana Sangh parliamentary party with drafting and other legislative work. Atal and Advani were great friends. They were both bachelors at that time (Atal never married and Advani only many years later). They would often go to see movies together in New Delhi's Connaught Place (now Rajiv Chowk) and spend their free time together. Undoubtedly a lot of time was also spent talking shop and confabulating on strategies for the party. Later, Advani became an MP himself. When Atal became the Jana Sangh president in 1968, after the sudden death of Deen Dayal Upadhyaya, Advani was close at hand to assist him in consolidating his hold over the party organization. In that way, Advani gave invaluable assistance to Atal and, when the latter stepped down after five years, he took on the mantle of presidentship after Rajmata Vijayaraje Scindia refused it. In the Janata government of Morarji Desai, both Atal and Advani held cabinet positions. They later launched the BJP together.

When Advani became the president of the BJP in 1986 and effectively the boss, Atal found himself marginalized. Those who know him say that he was despondent for a while but put a brave face on it. Advani, on his part, also showed him great respect. Efforts were made to persuade Atal to join the new opposition party led by V.P. Singh that was coming up to challenge Rajiv Gandhi, but he did not respond. This was construed as an inability to take a decision, but Atal's RSS background was too ingrained in him to allow him to jump ship. He might have been critical of some aspects of the thinking of the RSS but his way was to try to ensure that the shadow did not fall on the BJP, not to quit the party that he had formed.

Atal was not comfortable with the Ayodhya movement and would express his reservations in private conversations. But publicly he went along with the party. He had novel ways of protesting; when it was suggested that he become the leader of the party in the Lok Sabha so as to relieve Advani of the burden (since he was leading the Ayodhya movement), Atal refused. Possibly he had a premonition about what would happen in Ayodhya on 6 December 1992, and thus kept away from the holy town. When the Babri Masjid was demolished, he said that it was the saddest day in his life. In April 1991, however, Atal had told a VHP rally that the construction of a temple at Ram Janmabhoomi was necessary because 'national honour' had to be restored. Atal was arrested after the demolition but he held the Government of India responsible for what had happened, saying that it had not pushed for an early decision from the Allahabad High Court in the matter of 2.77 acres of land around the masjid. Had such a decision been taken before 6 December (when the masjid was demolished), kar seva would have started and no untoward incident would have taken place. This line of argument by Atal found an echo in the political resolution of the national executive meeting of the BJP in Delhi three weeks after the demolition. On 17 December, Atal also brought a no confidence motion in the Lok Sabha where he stated that the top ranks of the BJP, RSS and VHP had been trying to rein in the kar sevaks.

He added, 'I am ready to ask kar sevaks who were small in numbers to come forward and openly confess that they demolished the structure and face the music. I would also like to state that there were a large number of kar sevaks not involved in demolition. If the intent was to demolish secretly and according to a plan it would not require kar seva. Whatever happened there, we regret the incident.'

The Ayodhya movement seemingly increased the support base of the party but the leadership had to be changed. Advani himself realized that his image had become that of a hardliner and only a softliner could lead the party to victory. There was no acceptable face in the BJP other than Atal. Murli Manohar Joshi—who had led the party in 1991 and had organized an Ekta Yatra from Kanyakumari to Kashmir—did not have the ability to swing moderate votes, and neither did leaders like Sunder Singh Bhandari (considered very rigid) or even Bhairon Singh Shekhawat (who was closest to Atal in terms of ideology). Atal was the only credible choice. In addition, Atal belonged to the Hindi heartland and was a Brahmin. Till the turn of the century, being a Brahmin was a great asset for a national leader. Atal was one, but he did not take his sacred thread very seriously.

Atal's acceptability became an even more crucial factor in the run up to the party making it to the centre. For constituents of the National Democratic Alliance (NDA)—like Chandrababu Naidu of the Telugu Desam Party (TDP), Naveen Patnaik of the Biju Janata Dal (BJD) and Nitish Kumar of Janata Dal (United) [JD(U)]—Atal was the glue that bound them together. The BJP may have been the single largest party in the Lok Sabha, but without Atal no other party was willing to ally with the saffron party. Such was the stature of Atal.

Ironically, the problem that Atal faced was from his parent organization, the RSS. To insulate himself, Atal surrounded himself with liberal leaders in the BJP like Jaswant Singh and George Fernandes of the Samata Party. Brajesh Mishra—former secretary in the Ministry of External Affairs who was Atal's principal secretary as well as the national security advisor—was also a close ally. All of Atal's novel political moves were planned through this team. A close aide of his says that Atal depended on those whom he was comfortable with. He knew the dictates of governance and wanted the advice of those who were best suited for the role. The RSS kept up its pressure on him, demanding its pound of flesh in governance; but Atal kept it at bay, especially when Rajendra Singh was the sarsanghchalak. Rajendra Singh and Atal had known each other for more than forty years and this made their relationship easy. However, trouble mounted when Rajendra Singh completed his tenure and was replaced by K.S. Sudarshan. Meanwhile, a clandestine campaign started in some quarters in the party that Advani should be made the prime minister, because, after all, he was the leader of the Ayodhya movement that had popularized the party. It is this popularity of the party that had taken it to the doors of power. Sometime towards the end of 2001, Rajendra Singh (then already retired) was goaded to visit Atal and recommend to him that he become the president of India. Singh suggested that since at that time Atal's knee was troubling him, if he became the president, his life would become easier without any loss in his stature. Atal must have realized the motives behind the suggestion but kept his own counsel. Advani writes in his memoirs that the next day Rajendra Singh reported the matter to Advani. Incidentally, stories also started appearing in the press about the failing health of the prime minister, especially after his knees had been replaced. A particularly damaging piece appeared in *TIME* magazine, undoubtedly based on (incorrect) information supplied by political rivals. It presented a rather dismal picture of Atal's health, alleging that he had a damaged liver and one of his kidneys was non-functional. It also suggested that Atal required a midday siesta and that he was often not able to pay full attention during meetings. Obviously a lobby seriously campaigning for Atal's removal was at work.

Troubled days started for Atal after the Godhra riots and their handling by the Gujarat state administration. With national and international pressure being mounted on the Atal government to change the BJP-run Gujarat government, Atal was highly embarrassed. He decided to get rid of Chief Minister Narendra Modi. But, because of the pressure mounted by the hardliners in the party led by Advani, this could not materialize. Atal had to retreat; it was the first time in so many years that his leadership had been questioned. Soon thereafter, in July 2002, Advani was promoted to the rank of deputy prime minister from home minister; but he continued to handle the home portfolio. Sensing that Atal was now getting weaker, other elements in the party, not comfortable with liberalized economic policies, started questioning some of the reforms moves. Labour leader Dattopant Thengadi, who was the main architect of the Swadeshi movement, publicly called Atal's finance minister (artha mantri) anarth mantri from a public platform. This was an open demonstration of the differences within the Sangh Parivar regarding the government's economic policies.

However, Atal was able to balance the Ayodhya issue very finely. This was in spite of the pressure from the Sangh Parivar on one side and the NDA constituents on the other. In May 1996, Atal said: 'If the problems related with religion are not resolved for a long period of time, the result is what happened at Ayodhya.' On 6 December 2000—the anniversary of the Babri Masjid demolition—he said that the Ram Janmabhoomi movement was an 'expression of national sentiment that was still to be realized'. But a week later, under pressure from his NDA allies and also the opposition, Atal backtracked and got the NDA to issue a resolution saying that status quo must be maintained at the disputed site till the Supreme Court delivered its verdict.

He told Parliament, 'I never asked for building a Ram temple at the site of the disputed mosque.'

At the end of the same year, in his musings from Kumarakom where he had gone for a break, Atal clarified that the reference to the Ram temple and national sentiment was in the 'past tense' and that 'we cannot forever be shackled to debate on demolitions, either of the distant or recent past, India must move on'.

A party insider, who does not want to be named, says that the marvel of Atal was that he was able to maintain a studied ambivalence towards the RSS. 'He was with the RSS and against it also, all at the same time. Managing this was an art and Atal did this with aplomb.'

Atal's greatest achievement is, however, his move to normalize relations with neighbouring Pakistan. This was a mission fraught with trouble because of the internal power structure in Pakistan. Many analysts averred that the existence of Pakistan depended on the country maintaining continuing hostility with India. Atal had a bloody nose to show for his peace initiatives, his journey to Lahore in 1999 being reciprocated by Kargil. However, this did not deter him. He gave it back to Pakistan by evicting it from Kargil and again initiated peace moves. Atal was also not on the backfoot because of the allegations made by his detractors that the zeal shown by him was prompted by a desire to be awarded the Nobel Peace Prize and not because of any genuine interest in peace. The stories about his wanting a Nobel Prize started after then American assistant secretary of state for South Asia, Karl Inderfurth, stated: 'Leaders of India and Pakistan are certain to win the Nobel Prize if they succeed in implementing their resolve to live in harmony.'

The reality was, however, different. Atal's interest had been born half a century earlier when he began assisting Shyama Prasad Mukherjee on Kashmir affairs. When arrested at the border of Kashmir, Shyama Prasad had told his young assistant to go back to Delhi and begin working actively on the Kashmir issue. Atal knew through his deep study of the Kashmir problem that this was the issue that was central to relations with Pakistan. So when, as prime minister, Atal began to engage with Pakistan, it was primarily with the idea of resolving the Kashmir issue. To improve the country's advantage in the negotiations, he gave the go ahead for a nuclear test; although the advantage was lost because Pakistan conducted its own nuclear test.

Though Atal had acute political acumen, he made the mistake of allowing himself to be swayed by his advisors in 2004 to go in for early elections, eight months ahead of schedule. The advisors felt that Atal's moves had pumped up the economy and there was a feel good factor everywhere. It made sense to go in for early elections and win them with 'India Shining' and settle down to good work for another five years. The irritants being put in his path by the extreme elements in the Sangh Parivar were also playing on his mind. He felt that if he came back to power he would able to silence these elements. However, he had miscalculated. In the event, the government lost power and the knives were out for him. The RSS declared, 'The party has Vyakti and Vikas but no Vichardhara.' This was the RSS's way of saying that the party had projected a person (Atal) but not an ideology, and this was the cause of defeat. Atal himself was circumspect and when the RSS started saying that he should make way for a younger leader, he decided to quit. After all, he had reached the pinnacle of his glory. Atal decided to quit politics five days after his birthday on 30 December 2005. He had completed eighty-one years and knew that by 2009, when the next elections were to be held, he would be too old to occupy the top job. The oldest prime minister the country had ever had was his former boss Morarji Desai, who had come to office at the age of eighty-one. Atal did not reckon that anybody beyond that age could be prime minister. However, Atal remained popular in public perception. In 2007, *India Today* found in a survey that Atal was ahead of Sonia Gandhi and Manmohan Singh in the popularity stakes, and a favourite to lead the country. Obviously, many people were not even aware that he had retired.

After 2009, Atal's health deteriorated following a stroke that left him partially impaired and made it difficult for him to communicate verbally. The BJP, which made a bid for power in 2009, failed once again even as the Congress-led United Progressive Alliance (UPA) was re-elected to power. In the absence of Atal, it was Advani who led the party into the campaign. In the years that followed, the BJP felt an acute shortage of a top leader who could lead the party to possible victory in the 2014 elections. Advani, now himself long past eighty, was not willing to make way. Ultimately the RSS took charge and gambled on Narendra Modi as the BJP's prime ministerial candidate. Modi, as we all know, led the party to victory, securing an absolute majority for the first time in thirty years. The last time such a majority was won was in 1984 when Rajiv Gandhi romped home after the assassination of his mother. Incidentally, all this while Atal continued on the twelve-member BJP parliamentary board—the highest policymaking body of the party. Atal loomed so large in the party that nobody ever thought of removing him even though he was non-functional. However, on 26 August 2014, the parliamentary board was recast and Atal, along with Advani and Murli Manohar Joshi, made way for younger leaders. The three were made members of the party's Margdarshak Mandal.

Atal Bihari Vajpayee has now been awarded the Bharat Ratna by the government of his party. The demand for a Bharat Ratna for him is an old one. When Atal was in office, some of his associates had raised the clamour that he should award the Bharat Ratna to himself. This was after his success in the Kargil conflict. His predecessors, Jawaharlal Nehru and Indira Gandhi, had awarded themselves the Bharat Ratna, Nehru getting it in 1955 and Indira Gandhi in 1971. Atal, however, was not a man to do such a thing.

The demand for a Bharat Ratna for Atal was raised forcefully by the BJP for the first time in 2008 and again in 2010. Even L.K. Advani wrote a personal letter to Manmohan Singh, putting forth the demand. Stories doing the rounds suggest that Manmohan Singh, the then prime minister, was not averse to it, but UPA chairman Sonia Gandhi would not agree. Manmohan had thought very highly of Atal ever since the mid-1990s. Apparently, Atal had sternly criticized Manmohan in the Lok Sabha when he was the finance minister. Manmohan was so taken aback that he went to submit his resignation to his boss Narasimha Rao. Rao rang up Atal and requested him to appease Manmohan. Atal did this like a composed elder brother smoothing the ruffled feathers of a younger brother. Since that day Manmohan had begun to regard Atal highly.

The demand for a Bharat Ratna for Atal caught momentum in 2014 with not only BJP members but even former allies—like Nitish Kumar of the JD(U) who had worked as a minister for Atal—backing it. Although many expected that Atal would get the Bharat Ratna on 15 August, it was on his birthday on 25 December that Prime Minister Narendra Modi took the decision and got it approved by President Pranab Mukherjee.

The tragedy is that even though the Bharat Ratna has been conferred on Atal, it has come a few years too late. In his present state of health, suffering as he is from Alzheimer's, Atal is hardly in a position to understand or appreciate that he is now officially a gem of the country.

ONE

The Formative Years

IT WAS SOMETIME IN 1939, on a Sunday morning, when a fifteen-year-old Atal Bihari Vajpayee had gone to attend the weekly meeting of the Arya Kumar Sabha (the youth wing of the Arya Samaj) in Gwalior, that a senior worker, Bhoodev Shastri, asked him a question.

'What do you do in the evenings?'

'Nothing in particular,' replied the young Atal.

'Then why don't you attend the shakha of the Rashtriya Swayamsevak Sangh (RSS),' suggested Shastri.

Atal was quick to act on the recommendation of Shastri, whom he considered a great organizer and an intellectual. Unknown to him then, this decision was to change his life and set him on the road to one day becoming the prime minister of India. The Vajpayee family was a staunch adherent of Sanatan Dharma, i.e. orthodox Hinduism. Though as a sanatani, Atal would not be expected to have been exposed to the Arya Samaj, whose tenets are different from those of Sanatan Dharma, it so happened that the boy was introduced to the Arya Kumar Sabha, whose purpose was to cultivate character and a sense of purpose in young boys.

In those days, Gwalior was a princely state ruled by the Scindias.

In fact, along with Hyderabad, Mysore, Baroda and Kashmir, Gwalior was amongst the largest princely states in British India whose rulers were entitled to a twenty-one-gun salute, with only the Viceroy of India being entitled to a higher, thirty-one-gun salute. The rulers lived a life of luxury in Jai Vilas palace, the princes often embarking on shikars. The maharaja had a great fascination for electric trains and in the 1940s, he got 75m-long solid silver rails laid down on a giant-sized iron dining table in his central banquet hall. Trains ran over these rails carrying food during banquets. Needless to add, the levers were controlled by the maharaja. He could speed up the gravy train or slow it down as he desired. Life for ordinary citizens was difficult. The lot of the peasantry was unenviable. Yet, as in every princely state, the royalty was looked up to by the populace.

Atal's grandfather, Pandit Shyam Lal Vajpayee, had migrated to Gwalior from his native village of Bateshwar—on the edge of the Chambal ravines and on the banks of the river Yamuna—located about 70km from Agra. The village was in directly British-ruled India, in the United Provinces of Agra and Oudh to be precise. Shyam Lal's son, Krishna Bihari, was a schoolteacher and resided in the Shinde Ki Chavani area of Gwalior when Atal was born to him and his wife Krishna. It was on Christmas day, at five in the morning, when the newborn opened his eyes with church bells chiming in the background. Atal had several elder siblings; three brothers, Avadh Bihari, Sada Bihari and Prem Bihari and two sisters, Vimala and Kamala. Another sister, Urmila, was born after him.

Atal belonged to an ordinary Indian middle class family which relied heavily on education and culture in their children's upbringing. A Brahmin by caste, Atal had a belief system of high morals inculcated in him. His grandfather, Shyam Lal, was a Sanskrit scholar, and was fond of poetry, routinely peppering his conversation with shlokas. His father, Krishna Bihari, was also fond of literature and composed poetry in Khari Boli and Braj Bhasha. Thus, it was no surprise that the young Atal also developed a love for reading and composing poetry.

At a literary gathering, many years later, Atal said that in his childhood he was deeply influenced by the works of Bankim Chandra Chatterjee, Sarat Chandra Chatterjee, Munshi Premchand and Maithili Sharan Gupt. The writings of these authors were revolutionary in nature. The themes ranged from social revolution to political revolution; but all of them exposed the wrongs in society.

On coming of age, Atal was admitted to the Saraswati Shishu Mandir. As was the widespread practice in those days (and maybe even now), Atal's year of birth was entered as 1926 though in reality he was born in 1924. His father thought that reducing the official age of his son would give him two extra years of service; not knowing that his son would never be in service, much less government service where age mattered.

In 1935, Krishna Bihari became the headmaster of a government school in the Gorkhi locality of Gwalior; later he became the inspector of schools. Meanwhile, Atal continued his education and spent more time reading literature than the books prescribed for his courses. However, he was academically strong, and scored good marks. Yet his father felt that Atal was being pampered in school and once even asked his teachers to mark his papers conservatively.

As a young lad, Atal was not immune to the political influences of his immediate environment. In August 1942, the Quit India movement caught fire everywhere in the country, with top Congress leaders led by Mahatma Gandhi locked up in jail. Gwalior too did not remain isolated, though princely states were often less affected by the troubles in British India. There were demonstrations, boycotts and even arson in Gwalior. Atal, then seventeen, and Prem Bihari, his immediate elder brother, showed signs of being influenced by the movement. Krishna Behari was alarmed. He did not want his sons involved in political activities, especially as he was a government employee. To keep them out of trouble, he packed the boys off to the native village in Bateshwar—a peaceful pilgrimage centre commemorating Lord Shiva.

But such was the force of the Quit India movement that even Bateshwar did not remain an oasis of peace. On 27 August 1942, a ballad was being recited in the market at Bateshwar. A large crowd had gathered, and among them were the Vajpayee brothers, Atal and Prem. In the afternoon, two young men, Liladhar Bajpai alias Kakua and Shiv Kumar alias Mahuan, arrived at the site where the ballad was being recited and took centre stage. Liladhar also lived in Gwalior but, since his ancestors belonged to the village, he frequented Bateshwar and thus was fairly well known. Liladhar had come to the village a day ago seeking the local leaders. It so transpired that one of the Congress leaders had been arrested while the other had gone underground. Finding himself without any leader, Liladhar had taken the initiative in his own hands. He began delivering a charged speech in the market, asking the public to join the Quit India movement by breaking the law in defiance of the cruel practices of the foreign government. Liladhar and Shiv Kumar exhorted the collected crowd to follow them to the forest office where they could break the law by hoisting the tricolour and by ransacking the government office. So powerful was the oratory of Liladhar (who was around the same age as Atal) that as many as two hundred people (including Atal and Prem) went along with him. The crowd reached Bateshwar forest office and, led by Liladhar, began to demolish the building brick by brick. However, Atal and Prem did not participate in the demolition. Later, the crowd proceeded to Bichkoli to damage another office there; but the brothers again did not join them. The crowd declared that the forest laws of the British did not apply anymore and the country was free, raising the slogan, '*British, Bharat Chodo* [Quit India]!'

The incident, despite being small, created sensation locally. Soon the police arrived and made extensive and indiscriminate arrests. Both Atal and Prem were arrested and sent off to Agra jail where they stayed for twenty-three days. Liladhar escaped but was tracked down and nabbed a few days later from Agra. Krishna Bihari was alarmed to hear the news. His worst fears had come true. He had sent the boys to the village thinking that they would be safe there, but the boys had got themselves into trouble. He moved heaven and earth, looking for the right people to aid him in bailing them out.

Meanwhile, the police interrogated the accused to figure out the exact sequence of events. Statements were recorded before the magistrate. S. Hassan, a Class II magistrate, recorded the statements of the two Vajpayee brothers under Section 164 of the Code of Criminal Procedure (CrPC). The statements were recorded in Urdu, a language not known to Atal and Prem. Incidentally, statements made under this section could be used against those making them. Both brothers gave identical statements about the sequence of events and said that though they were part of the protesting crowds, they had not participated in the arson. The Vajpayee brothers were not prosecuted and their statements were not used in the court of law. Similarly, many others who had been arrested were let off. Liladhar was prosecuted and sentenced to three years of rigorous imprisonment. Shiv Kumar, his comrade in arm, was acquitted after being given the benefit of doubt because clinching evidence against him could not be produced in the court. A collective punitive fine of ₹10,000 was also levied on the village. This was a fairly large amount in those days. The incident continued to haunt Atal till he became the prime minister. This was because information would surface periodically, especially before elections, that Vajpayee had turned approver in the case, resulting in a young man (Liladhar) being sentenced to imprisonment. However, the testimonies of Atal and Prem were never used in the court. Moreover, many others present at the scene had reported and given statements to the magistrate that Liladhar was the ringleader. Liladhar, who by then was a retired employee of the Gwalior Municipal Corporation, was interviewed by *Frontline* magazine in 1998 on this issue. He agreed that the statements of the Vajpayee brothers were not used by the prosecution as evidence to nail him. However, he maintained that the statements could have helped to shape the prosecution's case at the investigative stage.

When Atal was arrested, he was a student of Victoria College, then known as the best college in Gwalior. Originally started as the Lashkar Madrasa in 1846, the institution was renamed Victoria College in 1887 to commemorate the golden jubilee of Empress Victoria. A new building was erected and it was inaugurated by Lord Curzon, the Viceroy of India, in 1899. In 1957, to commemorate the centenary of the first war of independence, the college was renamed yet again as Maharani Laxmi Bai College. Atal studied Hindi, Sanskrit and English for his Bachelor of Arts degree from the college. Since there was no college in Gwalior offering a master's degree, Atal went to Kanpur on a government scholarship to study for his master's in political science at DAV College. The college was affiliated to Agra University. Atal passed his master's with flying colours, securing a first class. After completing his postgraduation Atal took admission in law classes. Incidentally, one of his classmates there was none other than his father, Krishna Bihari. He was a man strong spirit and determination; and even though he had retired from service, he wanted to keep himself intellectually busy. For some time the father and son stayed together in the same hostel room. However, Atal could not complete his LLB as India achieved independence and his professional and academic plans changed.

By 1939, fourteen-year-old Atal had begun going to shakhas of the Rashtriya Swayamsevak Sangh (RSS) which had newly started operating in Gwalior. The organization had started in Nagpur in 1925, a few hundred miles south of Gwalior.

It had quickly spread in the Central Provinces, especially amongst Marathi-speaking people. Gwalior too had a large Marathi population—not surprising since the rulers, the Scindias, were themselves Marathas—and the RSS soon made inroads there as well. The boys who went to the shakha along with Vajpayee were mostly Marathis and, therefore, the swayamsevaks spoke in their mother tongue. This did not discomfit Atal. He enjoyed the physical exercises and games and especially the bauddhiks (intellectual discourses). In the beginning, Atal's father did not approve of this activity. On the eve of his becoming prime minister, Atal's sister Vimala told Rediff.com in an interview that Atal attended the RSS shakhas on the sly and that she, two and a half years older than him, would throw his khaki shorts over the wall for him to pick up from outside the house and go to the shakha. His old-time associates say that Atal would go to the shakha, come what may, such was his interest in the activities of the shakha.

Years later, Atal reminisced about his early days in the RSS in an article: 'A pracharak Narayanrao Tarte had come from Nagpur to start the shakha in Gwalior. He was indeed a superb human being, a very simple man, a thinker and an expert organizer. What I am today is the making of Shri Tarte. After him I was inspired by Deen Dayal Upadhayaya and Bhaurao Deoras. Gwalior was then not in the jurisdiction of Bahauraoji. But once he had come to Gwalior with Balasaheb Apte who was then the bauddhik pramukh. He was very soft spoken and we were drawn towards him. I had talked with him for a few minutes.'

The same year, Atal went to see the first-year course of the officers' training camp (OTC) of the RSS in Nagpur. Here he came in close contact with Apte. Atal had gone there to understand how the camp was being conducted. He had been invited because the management at RSS thought that he had the potential to take on leadership roles in the organization. Atal attended the valedictory function of the OTC where he caught a glimpse of the then sarsanghchalak or leader of the RSS, K.B. Hegdewar. A few months later when Hegdewar, popularly known as Doctorji, fell ill, Atal went to see him. This was an indication that the young Atal was drawn heavily towards the RSS. Years later, when Atal was the prime minister, Narayanrao Tarte told Tara Shankar Sahai of Rediff.com in an interview: 'Atalji's natural interest in affairs pertaining to RSS convinced me that he would be an asset in the organization.' Atal affectionately referred to Narayanrao Tarte as Mamu. It was Tarte who introduced Atal to the inner circles of the RSS.

In 1941, when Atal was in the final year of high school, he joined the OTC. The OTCs are conducted by the RSS to train their members to hold higher responsibilities, concentrating specifically on administering the working of shakhas. Till 1947, Atal worked for the RSS at the shakha level, independently running a shakha at a place called Shandila near Lucknow. He ran the shakha in the morning and later through the day composed poetry and sought the company of writers.

Needless to add, Atal was greatly influenced by the ideology of the RSS and the means by which it operated. In fact, in an article written years after his retirement from active politics, Atal said that the 'RSS was his soul'. He went on to say how the RSS influenced people's opinions. One incident recalled by Atal relates to his elder brother, who too went to the RSS shakhas. At a winter camp of the RSS, his brother, conscious of his high caste status as a Brahmin, told the camp organizer that he would not eat along with the others but would prefer to cook his own food. The camp organizer assented and gave him all the provisions to cook food. This he did for one day, but the next day gave up the idea and stood in line along with the others to partake of food from the community kitchen. Atal referred to the incident to explain how the RSS is able to break down social barriers and bring about a feeling of togetherness.

Even before he had joined the RSS, Atal was quite influenced by the Hindu way of thinking. This is clear from a poem that he wrote when he was in class 10. Titled '*Hindu Tan-man, Hindu Jeevan*', in the poem, Atal declares, '*Rag Rag Hindu mera parichay*.' Alluding to the temples vandalized in India by Muslim invaders, Atal goes on to ask in the poem: '*Koi bataye Kabul mein jaakar kitne masjid todey* [Tell us how many Hindus went to Kabul to destroy mosques?].'

He was also quite influenced by a book called *Amar Kirti Vijay Pataka* that had been penned by Mahatma Ramachandra Veer a contemporary activist for Hindi and for a ban on cow slaughter. Ramachandra Veer (who belonged to a region between Jaipur and Alwar in north Rajasthan) had argued in his book that the history of India over the last thousand years should be seen as that of 'struggle and victory' and not of 'defeat and slavery'. Most Hindu-inclined historians saw the saga of India from 1000 AD onwards as that of disgrace of the Hindus and their subjugation to the Muslims. Ramachandra Veer, however, gave it a positive spin in his book and this greatly moved Atal and apparently changed the direction of his life.

Atal was very interested in debating. In 1944, he went to debate in Allahabad. This was documented by Rajendra Singh, a lecturer at the University of Allahabad, who later became the sarsanghchalak of the RSS. Atal arrived late after his turn was over, but he requested the judges that he be allowed to speak. Atal said that he had been delayed because the train was running late and that he had come to Allahabad only to speak at the debate. By that time the judges had more or less decided on the results of the competition, but on Atal's pleading, allowed him to speak. Within a few minutes the tables had turned and the audience was enthralled. When the results were declared, Atal stood first. Two years later, Rajendra Singh recollected, there was a public oration in Kanpur which was to be addressed by a well-known leader. As was the usual practice, lesser-known speakers, amongst them Atal, spoke before the main speaker. The leader, however, once young Atal had spoken, felt no need to speak, saying that Atal had articulated very well all that he had wanted to say and there was no need for anyone to say anything anymore.

Apart from his eloquence, Atal was also known for his writing prowess. Therefore, the RSS decided to deploy him for journalistic work. This, however, meant that Atal had to give up his law studies. *Rashtradharma*, a monthly magazine, was started by the organization on 15 August 1947 from Lucknow and Atal was appointed its joint editor, working under the guidance of Deen Dayal Upadhayaya. Though a joint editor, Atal actually used to perform multiple roles. A regular contributor, he wrote under many pseudonyms; he was simultaneously a proofreader, compositor, binder and manager, Many decades later, Atal recollected that he was so engrossed in his journalistic work that he sometimes even forgot to eat. A few months later on 14 January 1948, on the day of Makar Sankranti, the RSS started the weekly *Panchajanya*, and Atal was appointed the editor of the paper. Both *Rashtradharma* and *Panchajanya*, however, had to cease publication abruptly owing to the ban on the RSS after the assassination of Mahatma Gandhi.

Soon Atal went to Lucknow and got involved with a publication called *Swadharma*. Later, Atal joined the staff of *Daily Milap* and shifted to Delhi in 1950. Another phase in Atal's life was about to begin. This was going to elevate him and set the track for future growth. Temperamentally Atal was a journalist and given a choice, he would have continued in the profession. What added to the romance of journalism for Atal was that he could influence the thought process of people and thus contribute positively to national growth. Atal himself recalled much later that being an editor had its own charm, for he enjoyed a high status and nothing made him happier than the compliments received from readers for a good article.

TWO

Getting into Politics

IN HIS EARLY POLITICAL life, Atal was greatly influenced by Deen Dayal Upadhyaya. About eight years older than Atal, Deen Dayal belonged to the same region in north India as him. He was a Brahmin like Atal but had led an impoverished life after his father died young. Deen Dayal had grown up in different places of north India like Mathura and Agra thanks to the transfer of his guardians. Like Atal, he too had joined the RSS and was impressed by the dedication of the organization. When the Jana Sangh was founded by Shyama Prasad Mukherjee in 1951, with the support of the RSS, a few pracharaks were seconded to the new political party. Among them was Deen Dayal Upadhyaya who greatly impressed Shyama Prasad. In turn, Deen Dayal was very taken with Atal, whose work as editor of *Rashtradharma* and *Panchajanya* had been observed by Upadhaya from close quarters. Deen Dayal averred that Atal, with his youth, energy and writing skills, would be of great assistance. Thus, the young man was introduced to Shyama Prasad. The president of the Jana Sangh used to publicly say that if he had three associates like Deen Dayal, he would change the political face of India. Thus a recommendation from Deen Dayal held great value for Shyama Prasad. Little wonder then that Atal Bihari soon became an assistant to Shyama Prasad, helping him in his political work, especially relating to Kashmir. In his autobiography, L.K. Advani recollects his first meeting with Atal in 1952, when the latter was accompanying Shyama Prasad on a train journey to Rajasthan to popularize the fledgling party. Advani says that Atal came across as a 'young, intense looking political activist, lean and imbued with youthful idealism and carried around him the aura of a poet who had drifted into politics, something was smouldering in him'.

When Shyama Prasad went to Srinagar to protest against the government regulations that allowed only those with permits into Kashmir, Atal accompanied him on train till Pathankot along with three other associates. Over half a century later, Atal recalled the journey in an interview to the Press Trust of India (PTI) in July 2004: 'When Mukherjee decided to violate the permit rule by entering J&K, we thought that the Punjab government would arrest him and prevent him from proceeding further. However, this did not happen. Later we learnt that the Jammu & Kashmir (J&K) and Nehru governments had entered into a conspiracy as per which it was decided that Mukherjee would be allowed to enter J&K but not allowed to leave.' Shyama Prasad Mukherjee tragically died in detention in Kashmir in June 1953, plunging the fledgling Jana Sangh into a crisis. Though someone else became the president, the reins of the party passed into the hands of Deen Dayal Upadhyaya.

In the same year, the Lucknow Lok Sabha seat became vacant after the incumbent, Vijayalakshmi Pandit (Jawaharlal Nehru's sister), quit her post when she was sent to the United Nations as India's ambassador. For the ensuing elections, the Jana Sangh put up Atal Bihari Vajpayee as its candidate. Atal was barely twenty-eight-years old then. Deen Dayal believed that as an assistant to Shyama Prasad, Atal had picked up the ropes quite well and was ready to be tried out in a parliamentary role. Atal laboured hard for the elections, addressing over 150 public meetings; but the Congress was then in its heyday and Uttar Pradesh was its stronghold. Atal Bihari came in third, polling close to 34,000 votes. The Congress candidate, S.R. Nehru, won with approximately 49,500 votes and Trilok Singh of the Praja Socialist Party (PSP) came second.

The loss of Shyama Prasad Mukherjee was a blow for the Jana Sangh in many ways. Not only had the founder of the party died, but so had an able parliamentarian and a fantastic debater who believed in calling a spade a spade. There was no one to hold up the flag of the Jana Sangh in Parliament and represent its viewpoint effectively. Even though he had lost the elections, Deen Dayal wanted Atal to be elected to the Lok Sabha at the next available opportunity. The chance came when the elections to the second Lok Sabha were held in 1957. Not wanting to leave anything to chance, Deen Dayal persuaded Atal to contest from three seats: Lucknow, Mathura and Balrampur. Balrampur was a little-known and first-time constituency in the Terai region in Gonda district of UP. Though it was part of a taluqdari under Oudh state, Balrampur's rulers were staunch Hindus. In fact, the All India Ram Rajya Parishad, which had won a few seats in the Lok Sabha in the first three general elections before merging with the Jana Sangh, was founded in Balrampur. Though the founder, Swami Karpatri, was a Dashnami sadhu, he had established the party with the support of the Raja of Balrampur in 1948. With the ruler, who had a strong influence on the electorate, himself being a staunch Hindu, it presented a favourable opportunity to Vajpayee.

Thus 1957 was a three-in-one election for Atal. Many years later, L.K. Advani recollected: 'I do not know what precisely prompted the party leadership at that time to make Atalji contest from three seats. But looking back it was Deen Dayalji's judgment that was responsible for that decision. Evidently Deen Dayalji was keen that Vajpayee must reach the Lok Sabha, even if that meant trying his luck in three places. Deen Dayalji clearly perceived that if anyone in the party could ever fill the gaping void left behind by the martyrdom of Dr Syama Prasad Mukherjee it was the thirty-one year old youth gifted with wisdom and maturity beyond his years.'

In the end, Atal won from Balrampur. He lost quite respectably from Lucknow but rather badly from Mathura, with his deposit being forfeited in the latter. In Balrampur, Atal got 1,20,000 votes, nearly 10,000 more than his rival Hyder Hussain. In Lucknow, he got 33 per cent of the votes cast. He lost to the Congress's Pulin Behari Banerjee who got about 41 per cent of the votes. In Mathura, Atal came fourth, polling just 24,000 votes. There were five candidates in all and the winner, Raja Mahendra Pratap, polled more than 95,000 votes.

Several years later, Atal recalled how in those days not many were interested in an election ticket given by the Jana Sangh party. Since a lot of Jana Sangh candidates lost their deposits because of lack of cadres and support base of the party, there was marked reluctance on part of potential candidates to jump into the fray on Jana Sangh tickets. In the 1957 elections, the Jana Sangh won four seats and Atal was appointed the leader of the parliamentary party. Even though he was in his early thirties, he was elected the leader because of his fantastic oratorical skills that could be pressed into service by the party to make its point. The time allotted to a party to speak in a debate was based on the number of legislators that it had. This meant that in a House dominated by the Congress, the Jana Sangh got very little time to speak—sometimes barely five minutes if not less. This put pressure on Atal to communicate in an organized fashion, presenting his arguments clearly, cogently and quickly, without beating around the bush. This in some ways made Atal an even better speaker. Though Atal was a backbencher, no less a person than Jawaharlal Nehru listened to his interventions with rapt attention. Atal recollected, in an interview many years later, how once Nehru gave a point-by-point rebuttal of the arguments made by him in an intervention. Vajpayee spoke in Hindi and so did Nehru while replying to the points made by the Jana Sangh Member of Parliament (MP). It was clear that Nehru thought highly of Vajpayee because he would make it a point to introduce him to foreign guests and invite him to receptions thrown in honour of the visiting dignitaries. Nehru once introduced Atal to the British prime minister, stating, 'He is a young leader of the opposition who is always criticizing me, but I see in him a great future.' At another reception for a foreign dignitary, Nehru introduced Atal as 'India's blooming young parliamentarian'. It is said that at another reception, Nehru introduced Atal as one who could be a future prime minister. In fact, the then Speaker of the Lok Sabha, Ananthasayanam Ayyangar, used to say that Hiren Mukherjee, of the Communist Party of India (CPI) was the best orator in English and Atal in Hindi amongst the members of the House.

Atal was much younger than Nehru's daughter, Indira, and, therefore, the prime minister had some paternal affection for him even though they came from different backgrounds and subscribed to different ideological beliefs. Shyama Prasad Mukherjee, who had been the Jana Sangh's leader in the Lok Sabha earlier, used to clash bitterly with Nehru on the floor of the House. Atal was too young to be pugnacious in front of Nehru, and his detractors used this to question his credentials. Balraj Madhok, his bitter enemy in the Jana Sangh, is quoted by *Hindustan Times* journalist Pankaj Vohra in his blog many years later, as saying, 'When I criticized Nehru in Parliament on [sic] the wake of the Chinese aggression, Vajpayee told me that I would never get elected to Lok Sabha again. Acharya Kripalani who was sitting nearby told me that do not take him seriously since he is Nehru's planted man in the opposition.' One does not know how true this incident is or whether it merely reflects Madhok's feelings about Atal. Madhok not only saw Atal as a rival in the party but also as somebody who leaned towards being a liberal. Perhaps along with the RSS, Atal was also getting influenced by Nehru and his policies and even his style. This feeling, amongst other things, had been strengthened by a little-known essay that Atal wrote in 1960. Ramachandra Guha, historian and public intellectual, writing in the *Hindu* on 4 July 2004, quoted from this essay to highlight Vajpayee's vision of what India should be: 'The Jana Sangh must be open to all Indian citizens irrespective of creed or sect. The decision to keep the party's doors open to all citizens is not prompted by any considerations of political expediency. The Jana Sangh holds that the state by its very nature is a secular body and therefore it should not align itself with any particular religion or sect. The party is opposed to politics linked to religion and also feels that religious institutions should confine their activities to their particular fields. In the partition of the country we have already had a grim experience of the consequences of mingling politics with religion.'

However, these views of Atal notwithstanding, the Jana Sangh was itself looked down upon by intellectual sections and this is clear from vice president Dr S. Radhakrishnan's reception of a Jana Sangh delegation of four Lok Sabha MPs which called on him. He feigned ignorance of the party, saying that he had never heard of it. This, of course, could not be true because the death of Shyama Prasad a few years earlier had created a furore in Delhi. For this reason, if not anything else, the vice president must have been aware of the party.

Nehru's positive attitude towards Atal was in evidence once again in 1961 when he decided to constitute a National Integration Council (NIC). The council was conceived as a group of senior politicians and public figures that would look for ways to address the problems of communalism, casteism and regionalism that were issues dividing the country. Nehru nominated Atal as a member of the NIC. However, by the time the first meeting of the council was held in 1962, Atal had lost his seat in the Lok Sabha in the third general elections. In what was a blow to the Jana Sangh and him, Atal lost his Balrampur seat narrowly to Subhadhra Joshi of the Congress by about 2,000 votes.

There is a story behind Atal's defeat. Although Nehru was fond of Atal, he was determined to keep the opposition leader-cum-orator out of the Lok Sabha for political reasons. The beautiful and energetic Subhadhra, who was a refugee from pre-partition Punjab and had worked zealously in Madhya Pradesh in 1961 after the first communal riots in independent India, was nominated for the Congress ticket. This was a surprising move considering Subhadhra lived in Delhi. Nehru also requested the actor Balraj Sahni to campaign for her. Balraj was then at the peak of his career and had made his name in the Bombay film industry. He was known across the country for hits like *Do Bigha Zamin* and was part of the left-oriented Indian People's Theatre Association (IPTA). Bekal Utsahi, a poet who later became a Rajya Sabha MP, recollected in a newspaper interview in 2014: 'Balraj ji stayed at my home in Balrampur for two days and the result was history where a political novice defeated a sitting MP. The hero had helped pull the crowds.' He claimed that this was the first time that a cinema star was pressed into service for electoral campaigning in north India. Incidentally, reflecting his soft corner for Atal, Nehru himself did not come to campaign in Balrampur, although he was electioneering in UP. It seems that even Subhadhra was keen that Nehru address election meetings for her, but the prime minister declined. Many years later, journalist Visveshwar Bhatt stated in an article that when efforts were made to persuade Nehru to campaign openly against Atal, he said, 'No I cannot. Don't persuade me. He is very much interested in external affairs.' External affairs was not only Nehru's pet subject but also Atal's.

However, Deen Dayal Upadhyaya could not allow Atal to remain out of Parliament. So, in the same year Atal was sent to the Rajya Sabha. To retain his position, Atal was made the head of the Jana Sangh parliamentary party. Deen Dayal did not want to lose the advantage they would have with Atal as the leader. There was now a familiarity with him in the top political circles. This helped establish the Jana Sangh in the upper echelons of power, the same way as organizational work helped ground the party among people. In the biennial elections to the Rajya Sabha, Atal Bihari was elected from UP and began his term in the Upper House from 3 April 1962. His six-year term was till 2 April 1968.

As a member of the Rajya Sabha, Atal was active as a legislator and, in 1966-67, he was elected the chairman of the Committee on Government Assurances. This was a committee of MPs whose function was to scrutinize the assurances, promises and undertakings given by ministers on the floor of the House and report whether these have been implemented or not. In 1966, as per official statistics, the government made 436 assurances on the floor of the Rajya Sabha and in the following year, 495. The Vajpayee-led committee found that all the assurances were implemented.

As a Rajya Sabha member, Atal went abroad for the first time. In those days, going abroad was not as commonplace as it is now, so overseas trips were a matter of pride. Atal's first trip abroad was in 1965 when he went to various countries of East Africa as part of a parliamentary goodwill mission. The next year he was part of the Indian delegation to the Commonwealth Parliamentary Association to Canada, and in 1967, he travelled down under to Australia as part of a parliamentary delegation.

Though Atal was an able parliamentarian, he was also a man of the masses. Little wonder then that the Association of Station Masters and Assistant Station Masters approached him and Atal became its president from 1965 to 1970. The association had been set up a few years before, in 1953, by station masters who felt that the railway heads were not heeding their voice because they were not part of the unionized staff. The president for the first few years was parliamentarian B.S. Moorthy, and after that Atal was invited to head the organization. After Atal finished his term, the body decided to elect a head from amongst themselves. This meant that the body had been empowered enough to not require an outsider to lead it anymore.

Atal's interventions in Parliament were in line with the nationalistic philosophy of the Jana Sangh. For instance, Atal was part of the the joint select committee of MPs set up to review the eighty-year-old Arms Act in 1959 where he gave a note of dissent. Atal's view and that of his party was that military training should be made compulsory for every able-bodied individual. This was to counter the 'expansionist' designs of the neighbouring countries. Atal felt that the new Arms Act, that came out of the deliberations of the joint committee, was not liberal enough in the sense that owning arms was not easy. In his note, he pointed out that the original act was enacted with a view to disarming the nation to safeguard the Empire and 'was motivated by a sense of distrust and an attitude of contempt to the Indian people' and these concerns were no longer valid.

In 1962, as an MP, Atal brought in a private member's bill to amend the Constitution to introduce Sindhi in the eighth schedule and thus make it an official language. The move catered to the interests of the Sindhis, many of whom were staunch supporters of the party. Prominent among them were K.R. Malkani and L.K. Advani. In fact, the whole Sindhi community had been agitating for recognition of Sindhi since the mid-1950s, but Nehru was not sympathetic to the demand. However, Atal's bill did not make the grade though it catered to the sensibilities of a people whose entire state had gone to Pakistan (unlike Punjab and Bengal that had been divided). In fact, Atal withdrew the bill because he realized that the government of the day would not allow a private member's bill to be passed. An astute parliamentarian, Atal realized that his role was to put the spotlight on the issue. A few years later, when the government had still not done the needful, another Jana Sangh MP, U.N. Trivedi, once again introduced a new private member's bill with the same intent. This time the government relented and in March 1967, it brought in an official bill to amend the Constitution to include Sindhi in the eighth schedule.

Even before India and China fought a war based on border disputes, Vajpayee was taking a keen interest in the relations between the two countries, especially with reference to Tibet. Speaking in the Lok Sabha on 8 May 1959, Atal said: 'When we accepted the sovereignty of China on Tibet we made a mistake. That day was an unfortunate day. Where has the Panchsheel agreement gone? Those who proclaim Panchsheel say that according to Panchsheel democracy and dictatorship can live together. If for the communist imperialism the peace and religion loving people of Tibet can't keep their way of life, then it is meaningless to say that in such a big world communism and democracy can co-exist. We don't want to interfere in the internal affairs of Tibet. But Tibet is not an internal affair of China. I represent a small party but our party defends the independence of Tibet. We want friendship with China but we should not build the palace of this friendship on the dead body of Tibet's independence.'

A few months later, on 21 August 1959, as the Government of India was preparing to raise the question of entry of China in the UN, at the UN session scheduled for 15 September that year, Atal moved a motion in the Lok Sabha. The motion said: 'The opinion of this House is that the government should send the Tibetan issue to the UN. By this motion I would like the House to suggest to the government to also raise the Tibetan question at the UN session.' The motion was defeated but Atal had drawn attention to a rather important issue.

In those early days, the Jana Sangh was faced with the paucity of funds. Established parties like the Congress had no such problems because industrialists were ever ready to oblige the ruling party. This irked the Jana Sangh which felt that a level playing field was being denied to them. Thus, in August 1962, Atal introduced a private member's bill that sought to amend the Companies Act of 1956, to bar companies from making donations to political parties. Atal argued on the floor of the House that those in charge of companies had no moral right to spend shareholders' money funding political parties: 'Why do companies want to donate money to parties? Do the owners of companies give money to political parties to show they are patriotic? Companies are set up for financial aims and there is no need for them to give money as donations. Political parties to whom they give donations malign politics. Money is needed to run parties but parties represent the people and they should go to people to collect money.' There was a furious debate on the bill and after discussing it three times, it was ultimately rejected on 27 November 1964.

Among other matters brought before Parliament, one was regarding adulteration of edible oils. Atal moved a bill on 17 August 1962 titled 'The prevention of hydrogenation of oil, seeking a ban on the manufacture of vanaspati in the country'. Initiating the debate, Atal said, 'The manufacture of hydrogenated oils [vanaspati] is on the increase in the country. There is a strong feeling that use of vanaspati is injurious to public health. It can also be used as an adulterant of ghee. Manufacture of vanaspati is also adversely affecting the development of dairies in rural areas. Total prohibition of hydrogenation is the only remedy. The vanaspati that is sold as pure ghee has nothing to do with pure ghee and its use in the country is increasing.' The bill received support from all political parties and the government agreed to bring in legislation to curb the manufacture of vanaspati. The government and opposition, however, took no action on it. The vanaspati industry had become too big with big companies like Hindustan Lever (with Dalda) and DCM (with Rath) in the fray, and they were able to convince the government otherwise.

After the death of Shyama Prasad Mukherjee, the Jana Sangh had come under the direct control of the RSS and the latter controlled the party through Deen Dayal Upadhyaya. But Deen Dayal was a self-effacing man and preferred to operate as the general secretary of the party. Short of men of stature within its ranks, the president was always an outsider whose thinking was in sync with that of the Sangh Parivar. The understanding was that the president would not meddle in the day-to-day running of the party and would confine himself to being titular head. From 1963–64, the president of the party was Dr Raghu Vira, a well-known Indologist who, thanks to Jawaharlal Nehru, was first elected to the constituent assembly and later to the Rajya Sabha. However, Raghu Vira had differences with Nehru on his policy on China. Shortly thereafter, Raghu Vira entered the Jana Sangh fold and became its president. However, he died tragically in a road accident, leaving the position of president vacant.

After asking Deen Dayal again, RSS chief M.S. Golwalkar decided that now that the party was over ten-years old, somebody from within its fold should be elevated to the post. The choice fell on Bachharaj Vyas, an RSS karyakarta from Nagpur. Belonging to Nagpur, Vyas was extremely close to the RSS heads, especially Balasaheb Deoras who was then high up in the RSS hierarchy and a few years later became its sarsanghchalak or chief. In fact, Vyas was a swayamsevak of the sangh shakha of which Deoras was the karyavaha. Though a sincere man, Vyas, besides being extremely self-effacing, had no knack for public affairs except at the organizational level. The RSS bosses thought that Vyas's personality had undergone a metamorphosis after coming in touch with the organization and, therefore, he could well be elevated to head the Jana Sangh. Deoras later remembered Vyas's 'metamorphic change' in a speech. He said that when he joined the RSS, Vyas had difficulty meeting and mixing with people. When he first attended a Sangh camp, he was not comfortable partaking of common meals prepared in the community kitchen and served to all. When Dr Hegdewar (the sarsanghchalak) came to the camp and was told about Vyas's problem by Deoras, he did not crack down on Vyas. Rather, he instructed the camp organizers to allow Vyas to come with his own utensils and give him grains and raw vegetables so that he could cook his own meals. For the entire duration of the camp, Vyas cooked his own food. But the next year, he went to Hegdewar and told him that he was a changed man and was ready to eat with everybody else.

The RSS bosses may have thought that Vyas was a changed man, but two upcoming Jana Sangh leaders thought little of him. One of them was Atal Bihari Vajpayee and the other was Balraj Madhok. The two were so incensed that they refused to attend the annual meeting of the party in 1965 in Vijayawada where the change of leadership was to be formalized and Vyas was to be installed as the new president.

The RSS chief M.S. Golwalkar was mighty miffed but could do nothing. Both Vajpayee and Madhok were important leaders of the Jana Sangh and he did not think it prudent to take any action against them. Next year, Madhok became the president. It was thus obvious that Atal, by 1965, had begun to feel and believe that he was an important member of the party and was ready to challenge the accepted norms of the Jana Sangh (a cadre-based disciplined party) if he was annoyed.

The influence of the Congress was waning in the 1960s. First there was the Chinese debacle in 1962, after which Prime Minister

Jawaharlal Nehru died in 1964. The Congress had been in power for seventeen years, and a lot of people had started becoming disenchanted with it. The opposition parties, not only the Jana Sangh but also the socialists and the Swatantra Party, were trying to make common cause against the Congress. The Congress's position was under threat in India's largest state UP, which had hitherto been a strong bastion of the ruling party.

Thus, in the 1967 elections when Atal stood again from Balrampur, he was unbeatable. He polled more than 50 per cent of the votes cast and beat Subhadra Joshi by a wide margin. Consequently, Atal quit his Rajya Sabha seat, whose term ran till 1968, and took oath as a member of the Lok Sabha. The Congress got a drubbing across north India and Samyukta Vidhayak Dal (SVD) governments cobbled together by opposition parties, and including elements from breakaway Congress factions, came to power. The Jana Sangh was part of the coalition and this enhanced the stature of the party. However, running the government was a difficult exercise because the parties that were part of the coalition subscribed to disparate ideologies. That the other coalition partners looked upon the Jana Sangh with suspicion only served to make the government more fragile. It required really great qualities in political management and flexibility to run the coalition.

When the Jana Sangh went to polls in 1967, the president of the party was Balraj Madhok. After Atal and he protested against the elevation of Vyas as the Jana Sangh president in 1965, RSS chief Golwalkar (who gave directions) and Deen Dayal Upadhyaya (who ran the party) decided to elevate Madhok to the top post. After all, Madhok had been the first general secretary of the party when it was founded in 1951 and a close associate of Shyama Prasad Mukherjee. However, everybody knew that Madhok was a hothead and spouted extreme views on most matters. This was hardly likely to endear him to other parties with whom the Jana

Sangh was trying to cobble together alliances. In fact, the joint front against the Congress had been opened up with a close alliance between socialist Ram Manohar Lohia and Jana Sangh's Deen Dayal Upadhyaya. The latter was a mild-mannered man, given to forging consensuses. For this reason Golwalkar used his moral authority to instruct Upadhyaya to take up the presidency of the party. Though this was something that Deen Dayal had been avoiding for many years, he could not say no any longer. Thus Deen Dayal Upadhyaya became the president of the Jana Sangh at its Calicut conference at the end of 1967. However, his presidency was not to last more than forty days, with him dying mysteriously after somebody pushed him out of a running train in Mughalsarai in February 1968.

THREE

Leading the Jana Sangh

THE SUDDEN DEATH OF Deen Dayal Upadhyaya brought on a crisis in the party. The late president had been handling the delicate task of managing the coalition partners in SVD governments in many states. Whatever might have been the constitution of the Jana Sangh, the ultimate call in the appointment of a new president had to be taken by M.S. Golwalkar, the RSS sarsanghchalak. A mystic-like man who remained connected to realpolitik in a strange way, Guruji (as he was hailed by his followers) did not control the Jana Sangh directly. It was only through a process of elaborate signalling, most of it behind closed doors, that the RSS boss operated. However, Guruji was in a bind. Whom should he nominate in Deen Dayal Upadhyaya's place?

Balraj Madhok, who had been the president the previous year, was lobbying hard. However Madhok, whatever may have been his commitment to the Jana Sangh, was not quite cut out for a job that required a consensus seeker. His personality was quite to the contrary. He was direct and shot from the hip. The other choice was Atal, who had made his mark in Parliament and was perceived as a moderate in a right-wing party in Delhi circles.

Atal's personality was eminently suited to managing coalitions. There was, however, a problem. Atal had given offence to Guruji by skipping the Vijayawada annual session to protest Vyas's elevation to presidentship. Moreover, not only was Madhok lobbying hard for himself, he was also actively campaigning against Atal. In fact, he called on Guruji and accused Atal of leading an immoral lifestyle. Guruji realized that, given the circumstances, if anybody could run the party effectively, it was Atal. Thus, setting aside the reservations that he had, he nominated Atal.

The fact remains that Atal had never shown Guruji any disrespect. Political scientist and Hindutva expert Jyotirmaya Sharma wrote in his biography of Guruji that Atal would never sit on a chair in Guruji's presence. On the contrary, he would make it a point to sit on the floor as a mark of respect for the saintly figure. When Atal heard for the first time that he was nominated for the post of president, he was shocked. 'How can I take the place of Deen Dayalji?' he wondered.

Atal's reign as the president of the Jana Sangh was not a bed of roses. L.K. Advani wrote many years later in his memoirs: 'Thomas Carlyle, the great historian of the Victorian era wrote that adversity is the diamond dust that heaven polishes its jewels with. Atalji was the jewel that shone on the national scene 1968 onwards.'

In order to run the party effectively, Atal built up a team around himself. L.K. Advani was a member of this team. Advani had been close to Atal ever since the late 1950s, when the former was deputed to assist the Jana Sangh parliamentary party in its legislative work. Advani was greatly valued for his drafting skills among other things. Other members of the team included Nanaji Deshmukh, an old RSS hand who had virtually initiated and grounded the organization in UP from the region of Gorakhpur. In fact, it is believed that it was Nanaji who had helped Golwalkar make up his mind in favour of Atal. Sunder Singh Bhandari from Udaipur region, an old RSS pracharak, was another member of the team. He was one of the first Sangh inductees into the Jana Sangh and had worked in UP. Jagannath Rao Joshi from Mysore, who was elected to the Lok Sabha from Bhopal in the 1967 elections, formed another important member of the team. Kushabhau Thakre, who had been appointed the general secretary of the Jana Sangh after Deen Dayal Upadhyaya was elevated as president, was another member of Atal's team. From the Dhar area of the Central Provinces, Thakre was firmly an RSS man. Also included in the group was Kailashpati Mishra from Bihar.

Political journalist Pankaj Vohra noted: 'Most of the supporters of Atal were from UP, MP and Rajasthan, especially the former two states. That is why it was perceived as a Hindi heartland offensive to marginalize the Punjabi lobby in the Jana Sangh that was led by Madhok.'

Years later, Madhok confided to Vohra that he was approached by Nanaji Deshmukh to not press his claim for the position. 'Nanaji said that a Brahmin from UP was best suited for the job at the stage that the party then was [sic]. Therefore it was in the best interests of the party to allow Atal to become the president.'

Balraj Madhok may have been denied the top slot in the party but he continued his campaign against Atal, opposing him on every possible ocassion. Madhok was, however, not successful in his efforts. Not the least because he was given to temper tantrums unlike Atal who was a cool cat. Atal was a moderate and Madhok mouthed extreme views at a time when moderation was the best policy. For instance, Madhok was president of the Indo-Israeli Friendship Society when it was fashionable in Delhi to be aligned with the West Asia lobby. He also espoused extreme views on Muslim issues. This was quite unlike Atal. Madhok's ego was perceived to have become quite swollen after he led the party to its biggest ever victory of thirty-five seats in the Lok Sabha. This was a record that the party never bettered in its Jana Sangh avatar. Madhok's ego obviously earned him enemies and Atal shone brighter in comparison.

Above all, it was Atal's lack of dogma which helped him establish himself in the party. Atal quite freely expressed the view that since there was no remedy for political instability at the centre (unlike in the states where president's rule could be used in a situation of political instability), 'the only readiness is political readiness of all parties to subscribe to coalition politics'. Not only had the Congress lost its pre-eminent position after 1967, a power struggle within, over the next few years, seemed to offer an opportunity to opposition parties, provided these parties made common cause. Deen Dayal, had been in favour of this tactical alliance with other opposition parties and Atal was of the same opinion and actively pursued this policy. This was at total variance with the Madhok line that 'if the Congress is malaria, the communists are plague'. By implication this meant that Jana Sangh should never ally even with socialist parties (which were closer to the left) although it would weaken the Congress. A story doing the rounds in those days (late 1960s) was that Atal had told Madhok in the past that if he had not joined the RSS in 1941 he would certainly have joined the communists. It was part of the canards spread to discredit Atal at a time when he had become a notable figure. A few years later, when Indira Gandhi started pandering to the communists, this was used to further show Atal in poor light, suggesting that he had an unwritten understanding with the Congress boss.

However, Atal, with his easily approachable ways, was able to surmount these problems. Not the least contribution to this was made by his appeal to various stakeholders in Delhi in those days. Rajya Sabha MP H.K. Dua (who many years later became advisor to Atal when the latter was prime minister) recollects an incident when, as a young reporter, he was going to New Delhi's Press Club for a press conference. The conference was to be addressed by Atal and, on the way, Dua saw the Jana Sangh president trying to flag down an auto, after the vehicle he was travelling in had broken down. Dua slowed down and offered Atal a lift, which the latter readily accepted. Atal, thus, pillion rode to a conference that he was going to address.

Sometimes, Atal's informal ways had the potential of harming his reputation. For instance, it was reported many decades later that a KGB agent masquerading as a journalist used to meet Jana Sangh leaders in a Connaught Place bakery called Wenger's. It was suggested that the KGB agent met none other than Atal. This event could easily have tainted Atal as a KGB agent, despite not knowing the said journalist. However, Atal as a leader of an opposition party, had no access to state secrets. At the most, he would have been able to share his perception of the political scene, something that politicians do with journalists all the time.

After initiating the split in the Congress, with a series of deft manoeuvres in 1969, Indira Gandhi was able to seize control of the party. As a result of this, the Jana Sangh performance in the 1971 elections fell below the 1967 levels. With the Indo-Pakistan war of 1971 leading to the creation of Bangladesh, Indira Gandhi's popularity had skyrocketed. This meant that the opposition parties were getting marginalized, the Jana Sangh included. Admiring Indira Gandhi's achievement in dismembering Pakistan, Atal compared her to Goddess Durga, who had vanquished the demons in mythology, raising the hackles of extreme right wingers like Madhok. However, those who knew Atal were aware that he was genuine in praising people when he thought that they deserved to be applauded. In the past he had openly admired Nehru when he thought that it was fair. It seems that one day, in the late 1950s, when the entire opposition was busy criticizing Nehru, Atal had stood up and asked whether it was mandatory for the entire opposition to criticize every move of the government just for the sake of opposition.

He had said that when it came to the integrity of the nation, everybody needed to stand by the leader, cutting across party lines. Similarly, Atal had been filled with grief when Nehru had passed away in 1964, declaring that the sun had set. He had said, 'Nehru was an honest man who was never afraid of negotiation and never negotiated with fear.'

At its executive meeting in its Kanpur session in February 1973, Madhok raised the banner of revolt, questioning the leftward drift of the party that he asserted was responsible for its poor performance. Madhok had in fact been raising the issue stridently after the party had lost in 1971, but this time he made the cardinal mistake of questioning the interference of the RSS in the Jana Sangh. Madhok had been an RSS man to begin with, but since he was finding less traction with the bosses with regard to Atal, he had begun decrying them in party forums. By now L.K. Advani had been elevated as the president of the party as Atal had finished a five-year tenure. Advani accused Madhok of party indiscipline and when party documents got leaked in the *Indian Express*, he was charged with being indiscreet and was suspended from the Jana Sangh for three years. In the event, the suspension was not revoked so it became a lifelong expulsion.

'However, Madhok's version is that he was framed. He said that the documents had been leaked to the press by the party leaders who were interested in getting rid of him. And when stories appeared in the press he was blamed,' says journalist Pankaj Vohra, who has extensively interacted with Madhok.

Vohra says that Madhok told him that he felt so humiliated that he stormed out of the venue and walked on foot along the railway line to the next station and boarded a train to Delhi. However, Arun Kumar, a political worker with the socialist movement (and later a member of the Janata Party), said that the decision to get rid of Madhok had been taken much earlier. 'At that time there was already talk of forging a common opposition alliance of sorts and I remember that our socialist party ideologue Surendra Mohan had communicated to the Jana Sangh as early as 1968 that Madhok was ideologically very aggressive and his presence would be a hindrance to the process.'

The oil crisis of 1973 gave the whole world a huge jolt. The Indian economy was severely affected by the cartelization of the oil-producing countries which formed the Organization of the Petroleum Exporting Countries (OPEC). Overnight, OPEC raised the prices of petroleum products by four times, throwing the whole world in a tizzy. In India, the wholesale and retail prices started going up, leading to across-the-board disenchantment. Foodgrains were in short supply. This further aggravated the price situation and inflation crossed 20 per cent. Matters became worse when the government decided to take over the wholesale trade in foodgrains. Labour unrest intensified, culminating in a railway strike in 1974. Things took a turn for the worse after a serious corruption case surfaced. A minor Congress MP, Tulmohan Ram from Bihar, was found involved in a scandal concerning issuance of foreign trade licences. He had apparently been set up by the foreign trade minister L.N. Mishra, who happened to be a major fund collector for Indira Gandhi. Mishra was shifted to the railways portfolio; but, a few months later, he was killed in a bomb explosion. Even as this was happening, a major unrest had broken out in Gujarat where students had taken to the roads, protesting against alleged corruption by the Congress chief minister Chimanbhai Patel, who was accused of taking bribes from oilseeds producers in return for looking the other way while they were indulging in black marketeering. Patel was forced by public pressure to resign but he let it out that he was only collecting funds for Indira Gandhi. The popularity of the prime minister who had been hailed as Durga merely five years ago was at its nadir. Old freedom fighter Jayaprakash Narayan, who had withdrawn from active politics many years ago, came back into the public realm and became the rallying force for the protesters and disparate political parties. Jayaprakash Narayan gave the call for 'Sampurna Kranti' (Total Revolution).

'Atal Bihari Vajpayee was greatly influenced by Jayaprakash Narayan,' says former union minister Jaipal Reddy who had been alternately in the Congress and the Janata Party. On his part Jayaprakash Narayan, who had been suspicious of the RSS (and thereby of the Jana Sangh) because of its alleged connection with the assassination of Mahatma Gandhi, began to trust the party. This was after Advani, at the instance of Atal, showed him documents that absolved the RSS of any complicity in the assassination.

As Indira Gandhi's popularity fell, she became increasingly authoritarian and showed signs of insecurity. Atal read the signals well and this reflected in the legislations that he sought to move in the Lok Sabha. Atal introduced a constitution amendment bill, seeking a three-member Election Commission in November 1974. The purpose of the bill was to provide safeguards to enable the Election Commission to function without fear or favour. As part of the same amendment bill, Atal sought that the selection committee for choosing the members comprise the chief justice of the Supreme Court, a member of the ruling party and one from the opposition. The bill was unfortunately not discussed and lapsed.

Earlier on in July 1971, Atal had brought in a constitutional amendment bill to ensure that the 'senior-most judge of the Supreme Court shall become the Chief Justice'. Atal was concerned about the concept of 'committed judiciary' that had been floated by associates of Indira Gandhi. Although a 'committed judiciary' ostensibly meant judges committed to the development of the country, most apprehended that it meant a judiciary committed to the ruling party. While introducing the bill, Atal said that the objective of the bill was to ensure the impartiality of the Supreme Court. He pointed out that in the matter of appointment of judges, the president was required to consult the chief justice, but in the appointment of the chief justice, the procedure was unclear. The bill came up for discussion in the Lok Sabha three times in August and twice in November 1973. When the bill was put to vote, it lost eighty-two to seven. This was not surprising considering that the Congress had a huge majority in the Lok Sabha but the low number of votes also indicates that even then parliamentarians were showing little interest in the matters before the House. However, Atal's apprehension turned out to be valid because soon a junior judge of the Supreme Court was appointed the chief justice, superseding three senior judges.

In August 1967, Atal had brought in a bill to amend the Indian Penal Code (IPC) that would make ministers liable for corruption by deeming them public servants. This followed the recommendation of the Committee on Prevention of Corruption. The bill, however, could not be debated and lapsed. Among the other legislations introduced by Atal, one was to amend the Constitution so as to remove Article 370 that gave special status to J&K. Debated in the House twice, the amendment put forth by Atal, however, lost in the voting.

Interestingly, Atal clashed with Indira Gandhi on the floor of the House. For instance, there was ruckus on the floor of the Lok Sabha about a strike of junior doctors in Delhi who were demanding ₹500 as salary and a separate city and non-practising allowance.

Indira Gandhi said, 'The poorest are not complaining and have not resorted to non-cooperation or hunger strikes. But the people who are complaining are comparatively better off. I am surprised. I cannot understand.'

Atal replied, 'Is there any special effort needed to understand this? The very poor are mute, unorganized and suppressed for centuries. They cannot fight. On the other hand those who are better off are aware and organized. They are adopting new ways of change.'

Atal, however, had clashed with Indira even earlier on, much before he had hailed her as Durga. On 26 February 1970, Indira Gandhi lambasted the Jana Sangh for its concept of 'Indianization' which is said to have been directed against Indian Muslims. She said she would deal with a party like the Jana Sangh in five minutes. Atal was mighty miffed.

He replied, 'PM says she can deal with the Jana Sangh in five minutes. Can any democratic PM speak like this? I say in five minutes you cannot even deal with your own hair, how you can [sic] deal with us. When Nehruji was angry he would at least make a good speech. We used to tease him. But we cannot do that with Indira. She gets angry on her own.'

Atal went on, '[Indira Gandhi] has not understood Indianization properly. Indianization is not related to Muslims alone. It includes 52 crore people of the country. Indianization is not a slogan but a mantra of national reawakening...But today secularism means anti-Hindu. Like non-alignment this government secularism has also come into suspicion. I take pride in my Hindutva, but this does not mean that I am anti-Muslim.'

Once referring to Indira, Atal said, '*Ekhom dwitho nasti* [there is no one but me]. When this feeling comes, it leads a person to dictatorship. Shrimati Indira Gandhi must be aware of this.'

Another time Atal said, 'It is easy to win elections by raising the slogan of *garibi hatao*, but slogans do not remove poverty.'

Yet another time, Atal referred to Indira Gandhi's government and said, 'Like a snake charmer who keeps his snakes hidden in a box, this government keeps its problems hidden in a box and thinks that they have ended. When the lid is removed the problem will raise its head.'

Things came to a head on 12 June 1975 when an Allahabad High Court judge, Justice J.M.L. Sinha, found Indira Gandhi guilty of electoral misconduct in her election from Rae Bareli in the preceding election, and barred her from contesting elections for six years after unseating her. Immediately pandemonium broke out across the country and the opposition stepped up the gas. Indira Gandhi, instead of heeding the call of the opposition to resign and taking into consideration the mood of the public, decided to invoke extraordinary steps and imposed Emergency in the country in the early hours of 26 June 1975. This, she claimed, was to maintain public order and ensure the integrity of the country. The opposition was accused of breaking this.

On that particular day, Atal was in Bangalore, where he had gone on tour as a member of the joint select parliamentary committee, considering legislations against defections. He was staying at the MLA (member of legislative assembly) hostel in the city when a little after eight in the morning, Advani, who was also part of the committee, came panting to him to inform that Emergency had been imposed. Advani told Atal that top leaders like Jayaprakash Narayan and Morarji Desai had been arrested to maintain public order and his information was that both of them would also soon be nabbed. After confabulating a while, both of them decided not go underground but openly go to jail. Soon thereafter, the duo went down to the dining room on the ground floor of the hostel to have breakfast. While having breakfast, they were told that the police had arrived and was waiting outside to arrest them. The two completed their meal and gave themselves up to the police, which allowed them to pack their bags and talk to assembled journalists before whisking them away. Atal and Advani were taken to a police station, where after waiting for hours, they were served detention orders signed by the police authorities in Bangalore. Thereafter, they were taken to Bangalore central jail and lodged in a newly constructed room in the yet to be opened hospital wing. The two were lodged together, while in a room opposite theirs, two other MPs, Shyam Nandan Mishra and Madhu Dandavate (who were also in Bangalore on that fateful day and had been arrested), were lodged. Atal took charge of the cooking for the four in the jail as food and cooking had long been his passion.

However, soon Atal was down with backache and severe stomach pains. This took him to the doctor many times till his ailment was diagnosed as appendicitis. Atal was admitted to Victoria Hospital and operated upon for removal of the appendix.

Even as all this was happening, Atal and Advani filed a habeas corpus petition in the Karnataka High Court. This was on the advice of their lawyer Appa Ghatate who found some lacunae in their detention order. The government also realized this fact and on 17 July revoked their detention. The release was only a token one, and within minutes, a fresh detention order was served on them. This time the order was passed by a deputy secretary in the Home Ministry in Delhi. A day later, Advani, along with Shyam Nandan Sinha and Madhu Dandavate, was shifted to Rohtak jail, close to Delhi. Atal was still convalescing from his surgery and was therefore medically unfit for travelling. Thus, he remained in Bangalore jail. Health problems continued to plague Atal. The back pain started recurring quite often and ultimately the Jana Sangh leader was found to be suffering from slip disc. In fact, he had been diagnosed wrongly. Perhaps the fact that he was a prisoner was responsible for the shoddy treatment.

Later, Atal was shifted to his home in Delhi and kept under house arrest. But since this did not improve his health, he had to be shifted to the All India Institute of Medical Sciences (AIIMS) in Delhi and operated on for his ailment in 1976. Atal had to personally write to Indira Gandhi, whom he knew well, for this shift. Many years later, this was to create controversy. When Atal was prime minister, the opposition claimed that he had written an abject letter of apology to Indira Gandhi to get himself out of prison. The BJP of course denied this, and its spokesman Vijay

Kumar Malhotra, said in 2003 that the allegations were 'lies' and that there was no letter of apology from Atal to Indira.

Businessman Sanjeev Kaul remembers having met Atal in AIIMS. 'My dad knew Atalji well and had met him a few times. Dad was a government official so he did not risk going to meet him in his official car. We stayed in East Kidwai Nagar, so he went to AIIMS walking. Once I too accompanied him,' says Kaul.

Writing in the *Asian Age* on 5 December 2014, a day after Atal was given the Bharat Ratna, minister Arun Jaitely said that the doctor treating Atal in AIIMS suggested to him, '*Aap zyaada jhuk gaye honge* [You must have bent too much].'

Atal replied in his poetic language, '*Jhuk to sakte nahin, yun kahiye, mur gaye honge; toot sakte hain, magar jhuk nahin sakte* [I can break down but never bow down].'

This poem, recollected Jaitely, was frequently heard during the 1977 elections. Insiders who were in the know say that the doctor treating Atal was sympathetic to him and deliberately kept him in the hospital for longer than required. The doctor did not want to send Atal back to jail. Since his word was final, he kept on asserting that his patient was not fit enough to be released from hospital.

Even as leaders like Atal were in jail, the rule of law was drastically abridged in the Emergency and citizens were deprived of their fundamental rights. Officialdom assumed extraordinary powers and political dissent was suppressed and freedom of press was curbed through censorship. Strikes were banned and no student agitations were allowed. Though industrial production went up and trains and buses ran on time, there was a deep feeling of discontent among the people. To complicate matters further, Indira Gandhi postponed the general election (that was slated in 1976) by a year and amended the Constitution, to include the concept of fundamental duties that were mandatory for citizens.

However, the censorship on free expression meant that Indira

Gandhi had no way of finding out the reality. She was dependent on reports from the Intelligence Bureau (IB) about the state of affairs. The IB, which itself had limited ability in gauging public mood, reported that Indira Gandhi would win the polls if they were held. Armed with this projection, Indira Gandhi announced in the third week of January 1977 that polls would be held shortly. She, being Nehru's daughter, was desperately seeking to restore her image as a democratic leader. At the same time, she released political leaders from jail. Atal's detention too ended.

Although they belonged to differing political ideologies, the opposition leaders quickly came together, bound as they were by the experience of the Emergency. Under the mentorship of Jayaprakash Narayan, they formed the Janata Party. The Jana Sangh merged into the Janata Party with other outfits like the Congress (O) and the socialist parties. At the time of the formation of the party, these leaders, including Atal, were not sure of their chance in the elections. However, they decided to give it their best try. This they thought would be their last chance. The Emergency was still on but the stature of these leaders had gone up with their incarceration. The public at large started viewing them with new respect and Atal, who also had his baptism by fire, found his popularity soaring. A rally was organized by the opposition parties at New Delhi's Ramlila Maidan. Nobody was sure how many people would turn up, braving the Emergency, at the huge ground. The government, to wean away crowds, also decided to telecast the superhit film *Bobby* on national television. In those days, the telecast of a good movie was perceived as a treat for the entertainment-starved public and attracted huge crowds at homes that possessed television sets. Belying such expectations, not only did huge crowds turn out and fill the ground, but people also stood on rooftops adjacent to the maidan. Many people came walking because public transport was packed to capacity. Atal was the star speaker and so he was billed to address the crowd at the end. It was winter and the sun had gone down by the time Atal's chance came but the crowd waited and lustily cheered Atal when he started to speak, raising slogans of '*Indira Gandhi murdabad, Atal Bihari zindabad*'. Atal spoke simply but effectively, telling the crowds how the whole country had been converted into a vast prison camp. He exhorted people not to vote for Indira but put their faith in the newly formed Janata Party.

In the elections, the voters responded to the plea of Atal and other opposition leaders and the Janata Party won hands down, notching a tally of 295 seats. Of these, ninety-three MPs were members of the erstwhile Jana Sangh. Atal himself had contested from the New Delhi seat and had won with a huge majority, polling almost 70 per cent of the votes. His opponent, Shashi Bhushan, a distant relative, polled just 28 per cent of the votes. In the 1971 elections, Atal had contested from his hometown of Gwalior and had won. But this time around, he had changed his seat presumably because it was perceived that he would have a better chance in the middle class-dominated constituency. The Congress party was decimated in the cow-belt states where it drew its strength from. Indira Gandhi and her son Sanjay, who were virtually running the government, lost. In the southern states, though, the Congress won a large number of seats. The Emergency was lifted even as the results were out, as Indira Gandhi did not want the provisions of the Emergency to be used against her.

Morarji Desai became the prime minister of the Janata regime. Though he was the tallest figure around, having been in politics since 1930, his elevation was not without a hitch. Dalit leader Jagjivan Ram had been part of the Indira government, but he had quit after the elections were announced. He nursed ambitions of becoming the prime minister and had apparently been promised by some leaders of the Janata Party before the elections that they would support his claim. Atal was said to be one of them. However, senior Janata leader Charan Singh made it clear that he would only support the candidature of Morarji Desai. At that time technically only Atal, as the tallest leader of the erstwhile Jana Sangh, could tilt the balance. After all he controlled 93 out of the 295 Janata MPs in the Lok Sabha. Once Charan Singh made it clear that he would only back Desai, Atal also expressed his support for Morarji Desai in no uncertain terms.

Thus, Morarji Desai became the prime minister and he appointed Atal Bihari Vajpayee as his external affairs minister. There was jubilation in the national capital as the public expected a lot from the government. Expectations were high from Atal and also his associate L.K. Advani, who had been appointed as the information and broadcasting minister.

FOUR

Love, Life and Poetry

Hum ne dekhi hai in aankhon ki mahekti khushboo,
Haath se chuke ise rishton ka ilzaam na do.
Sirf ehsaas hai, yeh rooh se mehsus karo,
Pyar ko pyar hi rehne do, koi naam na do.

Gulzar's immortal lines in the film *Khamoshi* aptly describe a very important aspect of Atal Bihari Vajpayee's life. Though not unknown to his associates, this vital part of Atal's life journey has been lived out of public discussions.

When Rajkumari Kaul died in May 2014, many newspapers reported the news. The conservative ones described her as Atal's household member but, writing in the *Telegraph*, journalist K.P. Nayar said, 'Mrs Kaul will be remembered for many years by those who knew her as the self-effacing, conspicuously selfless better half that Vajpayee never had and yet was always at his side till she fell ill and succumbed to heart attack.'

Journalist Girish Nikam, writing for Rediff.com, recounted his experience with Vajpayee and Mrs Kaul. Nikam, who was in touch with Atal for his reporting assignments (he was talking of the days when Atal was yet to become prime minister), recounted how Mrs Kaul picked up the phone every time he called up Atal's residence.

Mrs Kaul on picking up the phone would automatically say, 'Mrs Kaul here.'

Once Nikam, who had got used to Mrs Kaul's voice, answered, 'Yes I know,' the moment Mrs Kaul identified herself.

Mrs Kaul shot back very gently, 'You don't know who I am?' Nikam was forced to reply, 'No Ma'am.'

Mrs Kaul then replied, 'I am Mrs Kaul, Rajkumari Kaul. Vajpayeeji and I have been friends for a long time, over forty years. You don't know?'

Nikam wrote that he mumbled a reply, 'Oh I am sorry I did not know.'

Mrs Kaul then laughed and went on to say how Vajpayee had lived with her and her husband Professor Kaul all these years.

The only time the self-effacing Mrs Kaul gave an interview to the press was to a woman's magazine in the mid-1980s. When the interviewer asked her about herself and Atal, Mrs Kaul replied that both Atalji and she never felt the need to offer apologetic explanations to Mr Kaul once the dirty rumours began (of them living together in the same household). She added that her relationship with her husband was far too strong for that.

Sunita Budhiraja—a public relations professional, poet and writer—who knew both Atal and Mrs Kaul very well, recollects having called up the latter when she read the interview. But the phone was answered by Atal and Sunita said that she wanted to compliment both him and Mrs Kaul for the bold interview.

Atal said, '*Aap khud hi yeh baat unhe bataayein,*' and handed the phone to Mrs Kaul who was around.

Sunita, who was once close to Mrs Kaul but later drifted away, recollects that one day in a pensive mood she had confided in Sunita about her relationship with Atal. Apparently the two were in college in Gwalior at the same time. This was in the mid-1940s and those were conservative days when friendships between boys and girls were frowned upon. So, most of the time, emotions were never expressed by those in love. Apparently, young Atal left a letter for Rajkumari in a book in the library. But he did not get a reply to his letter. Rajkumari did in fact reply. The reply was also left in a book but it did not reach Atal. In course of time, Rajkumari (whose father was a government official) was married to a young college teacher, Brij Narain Kaul.

'Actually she wanted to marry Atal but there was tremendous opposition at her home. The Kauls considered themselves of a superior breed, although Atal was also a Brahmin,' says Sanjeev Kaul, a businessman from Delhi whose family is related to Mrs Kaul's.

He said that Mrs Kaul grew up partly in the Chitli Qabar area of the walled city of Delhi with her cousins before moving to Gwalior. She was known there by her nickname of 'Bibi'. Mrs Kaul's father, Govind Narain Haksar, was employed with the Scindias' education department. Kamini Kaul, a niece of Mrs Kaul's, but only slightly younger than her, remembers Bibi Behn's engagement.

'It was in 1947 around the time of partition and there were riots in old Delhi where we stayed. But Bibi Behn's mother brought her hurriedly to Delhi and got her engaged to this young college lecturer. The marriage was held later in Gwalior,' Kamini Kaul remembers.

She says that Brij Mohan Kaul was a very decent man: '*Bahut sidhey the.*'

Atal moved on in life but did not marry, and he became a full-time politician. The two met once again when Atal had become an MP and Rajkumari had moved to Delhi, her husband teaching philosophy in Delhi University's Ramjas College.

S.K. Das, an IAS officer who retired as secretary to the Government of India, has vivid memories of Atal in Mrs Kaul's house in Ramjas College.

He said, 'Professor Kaul was the warden of Ramjas College hostel where I was a student between 1965 and 1967 and a hosteller.'

He adds, 'Professor Kaul was strict and would land up in the hostel in the evenings. We were young students and we wanted to enjoy our newly found independence, sometimes imbibing a drink or two, and found the presence of the professor rather disconcerting.'

Das relates that after confabulations with some like-minded hostellers they decided to 'complain' to Mrs Kaul, who looked very friendly. When she heard of the 'complaints', Mrs Kaul was very understanding and smiled, saying, 'Why don't you come to my house when my husband goes to the hostel?'

The young students took the suggestion seriously and began landing up in her house every other evening. There they encountered Atal Bihari Vajpayee who was a frequent visitor.

Atal welcomed these young lads and engaged them in conversation even as Mrs Kaul plied them with sweets and sometimes even made thandai. Other than Das, the other lads included Ashok Saikia, who also became an IAS officer and was joint secretary in the Prime Minister's Office when Atal was prime minister; B.P. Mishra, who also became an IAS officer and was chairman of New Delhi Municipal Corporation (NDMC); and M.L. Tripathi, who joined the Indian Foreign Service and became India's high commissioner to Mauritius and Bangladesh.

'In those days we had no clue that Atal and Rajkumari had any friendship and many years later when we heard tales we felt very guilty for coming in the way of the two to be a sort of *kabaab mein haddi*,' says Das.

He is also quick to point out that Atal was never resentful of their presence and would encourage the boys to talk and was solicitous about their future careers options.

'In fact he would try to convince us that academics offered a good career and we should think of pursuing that. He also promised to help us get jobs. The Jana Sangh in those days had a strong hold over Delhi University,' Das reminisces.

These interactions between Das and his friends and Atal took place when the Jana Sangh leader was a Rajya Sabha MP and was already well- known for his oratory skills.

Das says that after college he lost contact with Atal and after becoming an IAS officer, he was allotted the Karnataka cadre. However, in 1978, when he was secretary to the Karnataka Chief Minister Devraj Urs, a visitor suddenly came over without any prior appointment to his office in Bangalore. It was his former warden Brij Narain Kaul.

Prof Kaul said, 'Atalji is remembering you and so is Mrs Kaul. You must visit them in Delhi.'

Atal was, at that time, external affairs minister in Morarji Desai's Janata government.

Posted with a chief minister close to Indira Gandhi, Das went to Delhi with some hesitation. When he went to meet Atal at his Lutyen's residence, Das found Mr and Mrs Kaul and their two daughters staying there. Sometime after Das passed out of college, Atal had moved into the Kaul household even when they were in the Ramjas College warden's quarters.

'Yes, we remember having seen Atalji living there and met him when we used to go there. In fact when she got old even Mrs Kaul's mother was staying with them,' says Kamini Kaul.

In 1968, after the sudden death of Deen Dayal Upadhyaya, the then president of the Jana Sangh, Atal's name was considered for the presidency. However, Atal had a strong rival in the party— Balraj Madhok. The latter averred that he was a better candidate to take over the reins of the party, especially because the Jana Sangh's creditable performance of winning thirty-five seats in the Lok Sabha in the 1967 general elections was under his watch. Moreover, he was the seniormost vice president of the party. Madhok began lobbying with the RSS sarsanghchalak M.S. Golwalkar, who wielded tremendous influence in the party. Among other things, Madhok also referred to allegations about Atal's immoral lifestyle and contended that there were complaints that women were visiting him. This was a reference to Mrs Kaul sometimes dropping into Atal's home to meet him. Atal even used to share his home with some other Jana Sangh leaders. The complaint, however, yielded no results because Golwalkar dismissed it.

Atal's unconventional lifestyle and his staying together with the Kaul family were spoken about in Delhi's political circles. However, the press never made a big issue of it and so Atal's personal life never came under the scanner.

The *Indian Express* wrote the day after Mrs Kaul's death, 'Both he [Atal] and Mrs Kaul never gave their relationship a name and whispered rumours apart, were never pushed to do so.'

In fact, reports on Mrs Kaul's death, in some sections of the press, described her as a member of the Atal household. This description was prompted by a press release from Atal's home that described her as such. Since Atal himself is suffering from Alzheimer's disease, he could not have had any hand in drafting the release.

'It was a rather incorrect description of her that Mrs Kaul would have been the first person to shoot down. Alas, in the hour of grief, somebody stupidly described her merely as a member of the Atal household. In reality she was the anchor of Atal's life, somebody without whose emotional support, perhaps the man could not have reached the level to which he rose,' says a person who knew both of them closely but would rather not be identified.

Of course, political circles recognized the importance of Mrs Kaul. Though she died when campaigning for the 2014 general elections was at its peak, top BJP leaders like L.K. Advani, Rajnath Singh and Sushma Swaraj attended the funeral. Narendra Modi was, however, held up elsewhere in the country. Significantly, Congress supremo Sonia Gandhi paid a quiet visit to the Atal residence to condole the death; even Jyotiraditya Scindia, the scion of the house of Scindias, who ruled Gwalior when Atal and Rajkumari Kaul were attending college there, went for the funeral.

Writing an obituary after Mrs Kaul's death, former Atal aide Sudheendra Kulkarni described her as 'Rajkumari Kaul, mother of Shri Atalji's adopted daughter Namita.'

In fact, soon after Atal started living with the Kauls, he informally adopted the two daughters of the family—Namita and Namrata. Kulkarni, who had been closely interacting with Atal for many years and had been visiting Mrs Kaul's home for years even before Atal became the prime minister, described her as a very kindly woman, whose face was motherly and whose heart was motherly.

Kulkarni added, 'Those who interacted with her found her very cultured in a very profound and multi-dimensional sense.'

'Of all the members of every prime ministerial household since Independence, Auntie (as she was known to those who had privileged access to her home) was the most understated but her worth was known to those who knew the intricacies of the organogram of Atal's private life,' wrote K.P. Nayar in the *Telegraph*. He added that with the death of Mrs Kaul, 'the greatest love story of Indian politics ended forever in as subdued a style as it flourished for several decades under the radar but was known widely'.

In the same vein, senior journalist Pankaj Vohra, who has been a keen observer of Delhi's political scene, told this author, 'Mrs Kaul was the fulcrum around which the Atal household functioned. When Atal became the prime minister, the boys from Ramjas College who knew him from their student days gained prominence. In fact Ramjas Club became a term used in Delhi in those days. But remember that these boys were very close to Mrs Kaul and less so to Atal. They came to be known because of Mrs Kaul.'

S.K. Das also seems to ratify this view indirectly when he says, 'For most of us staying outside Delhi but visiting the Atal household when in the capital, the attraction was to meet Mrs Kaul rather than Atal himself.'

When Atal became prime minister, his first private secretary was Shakti Sinha, an IAS officer of the union territory cadre. Sinha's wife, an Indian Revenue Service (IRS) officer, was the niece of Mrs Kaul. Sinha was the secretary to Atal even before Atal was the leader of the opposition. Incidentally, when Sinha left his job for a World Bank assignment, he had his junior V. Anandrajan elevated to the position. Anandrajan, a relatively junior IRS officer at that time, was yanked out of his modest job to be put in the Prime Minister's Office for the simple reason that he knew Shakti Sinha from before. Anandrajan's wife was reporting to Shakti Sinha's wife in the income tax department.

'It is thus that the Mrs Kaul angle worked in the Atal regime. As another example, another IAS officer P.K. Hota became important in the Atal regime. He was not from Ramjas College but was a hosteller in the neighbouring Kirori Mal College of Delhi University and was friends with the boys who formed the core of the Ramjas Club,' says Pankaj Vohra.

There was a change in the Atal household in the early 1980s when his adopted daughter (and Mrs Kaul's daughter) Namita got married to Ranjan Bhattacharya. The latter was a Bengali from Patna who was working for the Oberoi hotel in Delhi when his romance with Namita blossomed in the early 1980s. She had passed out of Delhi University's Daulat Ram College and was working in Maurya hotel at that time. They had met earlier in 1977, during their university days. Soon Ranjan had started visiting the Atal household, but Atal maintained a distance from him even if they were at the dining table together. Though Ranjan and Namita lost their hearts to each other, a crucial test lay before Ranjan. He had to win the approval of Atal Bihari Vajpayee himself before he could marry Ghunnu (Namita's nickname). As Ranjan recollected in an interview later, Atal used to forget his name every time he met him and would address him variously as Banerjee, Mukherjee and even Bengali babu. Needless to add, the smooth-talking Ranjan, the very epitome of a marketing man, passed the Atal test and became part of the household. After marriage, he moved into the house and this may be partly due to the fact that Ranjan, although from a well-to-do family, had lost both his parents in quick succession while he was still in his twenties. Like his wife, Ranjan also began calling Atal 'Baapji' and, in fact, became extremely close to him. Ranjan soon left his job and became an entrepreneur in 1987. He built and ran a hotel in Manali for a few years. Later, he set up a marketing company that provided reservations to the US-based Carlson Hotels Worldwide. After that, Ranjan became the managing director of Country Development and Management Services, a joint venture involving Carlson and Chanakya hotels, providing budget hotels in different locations. Clearly, the career of the adopted son-in-law flourished after he became a part of Baapji's family, but then Baapji himself also used to repose a lot of faith in Ranjan. Evidence of this came when Atal was appointed as prime minister for the first time in 1996. His government lasted merely thirteen days but even in that period, Atal had appointed Ranjan as his officer on special duty (OSD). During Atal's later stints as prime minister, including the five-year one from 1999 to 2004, Ranjan had no official position but was widely known as a mover and shaker in Delhi's political and business circles. There would be regular stories in the media about the alleged deals being struck by Ranjan, though the son-in-law always denied them and asserted that he had nothing to do with the government. He agreed that he lived with the prime minister in his official residence, but, according to him, there was nothing wrong with that. After all he had been staying with Atal since 1983 and, therefore, there was nothing amiss with his moving into the prime minister's residence once Baapji became the PM, Ranjan was quoted as saying in media interviews. Ranjan also pointed out that he conducted his own business from his office in Greater Kailash and not the PM's residence in Race Course Road. Mrs Kaul's elder daughter Namrata became a doctor and ultimately moved to New York where she lives even now. Her father Brij Narain Kaul spent his last days with her. He had gone there for better medical treatment. This was much before Atal became prime minister.

K.P. Nayar of the *Telegraph* wrote in his obituary of Mrs Kaul, 'The only demand she made on Vajpayee when he went to the UN in New York for annual general assembly was that he should adjust his travel dates so that he could be in the US on the birthday of Namrata.' Nayar also wrote, 'Mrs Kaul never figured in PM's protocol books as hostess at official programmes and did not travel with Vajpayee on his foreign trips but her unseen presence was evident during all such trips.' He added, 'Bhattacharya, who almost always accompanied the PM abroad at times with Namita and were listed in the protocol book as family was often reminded by Mrs Kaul on his cell phone when it was time for Vajpayee to take medicines.'

Atal Bihari Vajpayee belonged to an ordinary middle class family. Though he made it big in politics, his siblings remained moored in their middle class existence. Atal's elder brother, Awadh Bihari, retired as a deputy secretary to the government of Madhya Pradesh in 1997. Another of his brothers, Sada Bihari, ran a book publishing business in Gwalior. However, his daughter Karuna Shukla joined the BJP and even became an MLA. Prem Bihari, who was closest to Atal, joined the Co-operation Department of the Government of Madhya Pradesh, and was posted in Bilaspur. When Atal became prime minister, Prem Bihari's son, Navin, recounted the story of a holiday they took in Delhi many years ago, to Rediff.com. He said that when they reached Delhi and alighted from the train, their father sent Navin's elder brother to Atal's home to find out whether he was around. Atal was by that time already a prominent politician. The rest of the family stayed in the retiring room at the station. Atal, on hearing that his brother and family had come to Delhi, immediately rushed to the station and took them home. Navin recollected that they were very hesitant about carrying a matka of water that they had with them in the taxi, but Atal, who was Chote Chachaji for his nephews, put everybody at ease by saying that a matka cooled water better than a fridge, and he himself carried the matka to the taxi.

In the same interview, other nephews of Atal said that their uncle was close to the family and would not miss out on important family functions like marriages. However, they also said that Atal never went out of his way to do favours for his family members. It seemed that Prem Bihari had sought to stall his transfer when the first non-Congress government was ruling in Madhya Pradesh. Although the minister concerned, Arif Baig, was from the BJP, Atal did not oblige. Atal's sister Urmila Mishra reminisced, in the same interview, that there were a lot of favour seekers and therefore they just forwarded the requests to him and did not pester him any further. Many of the requests were related to help in making a passport or admission in hospitals like AIIMS in New Delhi. Urmila's son, Anup, joined politics and was a BJP MP. In the 2014 general elections, he lost at the polls. Anup, however, was close to Atal all through. 'Even when he was the prime minister, Anup would drop in to meet his Chote Mamaji and so many times I have seen him at 3 RCR having breakfast or dinner,' says a close aide of Atal's when he was PM.

When Atal first came to Delhi in 1950, he was ready to stay

just about anywhere. Of course, then a total nonentity he could afford to roam around the city and go to sleep anywhere. It is rumoured that once he even spent the night on the lawns adjoining India Gate. After he became an MP, Atal, along with some BJP functionaries, moved into a house. Later, he was staying with Deen Dayal Upadhyaya, Jagdish Prasad Mathur and Dattopant Thengadi—all Jana Sangh leaders with an RSS background. Since it was a kind of community living with all bachelors, the household work had to be divided amongst them. Atal was in charge of the kitchen since he was fond of cooking and eating. He used to excel in making some dishes like khichdi and kheer. L.K. Advani said in an interview many years later, when Atal was PM and he deputy PM, how in those days, even till the mid-1970s, they used to go together to Regal cinema to watch movies. After the movie, they would often go and eat paani puri.

Had he not become a politician, Atal might have become a top-rated poet. As he wrote in the introduction to his poetry collection, *Meri Ekyavan Kativatayen* (My Fifty-one Poems), his political work and before that journalistic work did not allow him to concentrate on his poetry with the passion that he would have liked.

In the same introduction Atal wrote that because of the literary environment in his home (his father's written poem formed part of the prayers at schools in Gwalior area), he had started attending kavi sammelans from a young age in the company of his elder brothers. First as a listener and later as a poet. Atal said that the first poem he wrote (or rather remembers having written) was on the Taj Mahal. It was not on the beauty of Taj Mahal or the love of Shah Jahan for Mumtaz Mahal but on the exploitation of labourers who built the magnificent monument. The first few lines of the poem read:

> *Yeh Taj Mahal, Yeh Taj Mahal,*
> *Yamuna ki roti dhar vikal,*
> *Kal-kal chal chal,*
> *Kal-kal chal chal,*
> *Jab Hindustan roya sakal,*
> *Tab bana paya Taj Mahal,*
> *Yeh Taj Mahal, Yeh Taj Mahal.*

One of his best-known poems, 'Oonchai' (Height) was written when he got the Padma Vibhushan in 1992. It ended with the lines:

> *Mere Prabhu,*
> *Mujhe itni unchai kabhi mat dena,*
> *Gairon ko gale na laga sakoo,*
> *Itni rukhai mat dena.*

> [My Lord,
> Never let me climb so high that I can't bend down to embrace another human,
> Deliver me from such arrogance.]

Leading Indian poet and Jnanpith awardee Sitakant Mahapatra, who has translated Atal's poetry into Odia says that the former prime minister may not have been an excellent poet, but he was certainly a very good poet. 'He was unable to hone his skills because of his demanding political career. Otherwise he would have been a very noted poet. But he is a sensitive poet no doubt,' Mahapatra says.

Sunita Budhiraja says that he had limited popularity as a poet because he specialized in writing poems with 'rashtra bhakti' as the theme. 'After independence poems with these themes did not work,' she says, adding, 'had he been a hasya kavi or if he wrote on themes like love he would have been rated very highly.'

Atal himself has said many times that his political work restricted the poet in him. In a telling comment rendered in poetic fashion, he told Rajat Sharma in an episode of *Aap ki Adalat* in the run up to his becoming prime minister, '*Rajneeti ke registan mein, kavita ki dhara sookh gayee hai.*' Interestingly, in the same programme, Atal revealed that sometimes he felt that he should become a full-time poet but '*kambal chodta hi nahin*'.

In one of his poems entitled, '*Kaun Kaurava, Kaun Pandava?*' Atal asks how to distinguish between the armies of the ethical and those of the unscrupulous? The corrupt genius of Shakuni is being used by both sides equally. Dharmaraj Yudhishtira, the righteous one, is still a slave to the dice and Draupadi is still being shamelessly violated in every assembly. The Mahabharata is imminent. This time the great war will be fought godless, without Krishna the saviour. Victory might belong to either side, but the only loser will be the man on the street, the poem asserts.

In yet another poem he is in an absolutely contemplative mood. '*Kya khoya kya paya jag mein; milte aur bichadte mag mein; mujhe kisi se nahin hai shikayat; yadyapi chala gaya pag pag mein; ek dhrishti beeti paar daalein, yaadon ki potli tatoley.*'

One of Atal's best-known poems is '*Geet Naya Gaata Hoon*' (I Sing a New Song). The poem begins with the protagonist in a crestfallen mood saying, '*Geet nahin gaata hoon* [I do not sing]', and further, '*Benakaab chehre hain, daag bade gehre hain; toota tilism, aaj, sach se bhaya khata hoon, geet nahin gata hoon.*' In the second stanza, the protagonist has regained his confidence and says, '*Geet naya gata hoon; toote hue taaron se, phoote vasanti swar; paththar ki chaati mein ug aaya nav ankur.*' It ends, '*Kaal ke kapal par likhta, mitata hoon.*'

Some of his verses were sung by ghazal maestro Jagjit Singh in an album titled *Samvedana*, which was released in 2002 and included some interesting poems. There was one written after completion of one year of the Emergency, '*Ek Baras Beet Gaya*'. Another is

'*Jeevan Beet Chala*', a poem he wrote on his birthday. Admitted to AIIMS, he once heard the cries of relatives of patients who had died, resulting in '*Door Koi Rota Hai*'.

Atal may not have found much time to write poems, but he was very fond of attending kavi goshtis. Budhiraja says that political ideologies and party affiliations did not prevent Atal from going to poetry-reading sessions organized by rival party members. 'He required just a nudge to attend these poetry-reading sessions and I have seen him at the home of Congressmen like Bhagwat Jha Azad and Girija Vyas or at the home of socialists like Ladli Mohan Nigam. For him poetry was above politics.'

Atal was a regular in the company of Dharamvir Bharati, the editor of *Dharamyug*, who was also a leading writer. Those who have heard Atal reciting poetry say that the BJP chief was a great orator while delivering political speeches but his recitation of poetry was even better. 'He brought in feelings in his recitation and made up for what the poetry may have lacked in its contents. He gesticulated and paused at the right places to breathe life in the poems. He was a good poet, although not in the league of Harivansh Rai Bachchan or Sumitra Nandan Pant,' says a poet who has evaluated Atal's poetry but does not want to be named.

'What was great about his poetry was that they were straight from the heart. The poems were not contrived. His optimism was also reflected in his poetry and if there was a line or two denoting pessimism, the next lines would bring out optimism,' says poet Surendra Sharma who has recited poems along with Atal at both private gatherings and in public ones where Atal was chief guest. 'He would recite poetry in kavi goshtis before private audiences and would come there as an aam aadmi and not as a public person. He would have no hang ups,' Sharma adds.

Not only was Atal appreciative of good poetry written by others, he was also ready to compliment the poets. Sunita Budhiraja remembers how her poetry was published in the same edition of *Dharamyug* that carried a poem of Atal's. 'I felt very proud and more so when he called me and said that he had read my poem and loved it,' she says.

At the beginning of 2004, BJP leader and then minister of state in the Prime Minister's Office, Vijay Goel, compiled a list of his boss's favourites. Atal's favourite poets included in this list were Harivansh Rai Bachchan, Suryakant Tripathi 'Nirala', Balkrishna Sharma Naveen, Shivmangal Singh Suman and Faiz Ahmed Faiz. Atal said that the best movies he had seen in Hindi included *Devdas, Bandini, Teesri Kasam, Mausam, Mamta* and *Aandhi* and the best English movies that he had seen were *Bridge over the River Kwai, Born Free* and *Gandhi*.

Other than poetry, Atal was also fond of classical music, especially renditions by Bhimsen Joshi, Amjad Ali Khan and Hari Prasad Chaurasia. Sitakant Mahapatra remembers how he attended a recital organized by Atal at his residence while he was prime minister. 'This only shows his love for traditional music,' says Mahapatra.

Atal himself has talked in interviews about his love for shastriya sangeet and also about being moved by Meera's bhajans. One of his aides says that he was very fond of recitals by Kumar Gandharva.

Atal was born a vegetarian but later in life he became fond of non-vegetarian food and Chinese cuisine became his favourite. However, traditional Indian food like khichdi, poori-kachauri, and dahi-pakori delighted him. 'He is a great one for good food,' says one of his former aides. 'He found sweets irresistible and I remember seeing him gobble sweets when we used to visit him as students fifty years ago,' recollects S.K. Das.

In the compilation made by Vijay Goel, kheer, malpua and mangauri were listed as Atal's favourites. Admittedly, over the years, as he became older, his food intake reduced as he became more health conscious. In his earlier political career, Atal was fond of whiskey and made no bones about imbibing drink. By the time he became prime minister, he was seventy-three and he had given up drinking.

Those who know Atal closely say that he is a man of great depth and oftentimes his speeches and actions reflected his poetic and other deep thoughts. A good example of this is that when the BJP came into being, Atal zeroed in on the kamal, lotus, as the symbol for the party. Just as the lotus grows in mud but is itself untainted by the muck around, he wanted the BJP to be a party of principles, above the muck in politics.

FIVE

The Man and His Style

HE MIGHT HAVE BEEN the prime minister of the country, but he was a parliamentarian first and then the PM, asserts a former aide of Atal's. In support of this, he cites the fact that Vajpayee would almost always go to his office in Parliament when both the Lok Sabha and Rajya Sabha were in session, quite unlike most other PMs, to keep a close watch on what was happening, and would also intervene in the session when required. The aide, who requested anonymity when he spoke to the author, said that when the quorum bell in the House would ring (signalling that there weren't enough MPs in the House), Vajpayee would rush to the House. 'He was a man who took his duty as a law maker seriously, not surprising considering that he had been in Parliament for over forty years before he became the PM,' the aide confided.

Little wonder then that Atal was given the outstanding parliamentarian award in 1994, the second person to be conferred this honour after Indrajit Gupta. Jaipal Reddy, former union minister, who too won the outstanding parliamentarian award some years later, agrees that Atal's first love was Parliament and the rest was all secondary.

'I chanced to meet him in 1985, a few months after he lost the elections. His spirits were down and he told me that to be in Parliament meant a lot to him,' says Reddy.

His secretary for three years, Shakti Sinha, recollects that Atal used to do extensive research for his speeches in Parliament; including even those that he delivered extempore. 'He used to jot down notes, write ideas and make points,' says Sinha.

In Parliament, as an MP, he would often raise issues that would never occur to anybody else. For instance, when Pranab Mukherjee was first appointed finance minister in January 1982, Atal wrote to the speaker of the Lok Sabha, complaining about the appointment. The burden of his argument was that Pranab was a Rajya Sabha MP and, being a member of the Upper House, was not entitled to vote on financial, budgetary and public expenditure proposals. However, it is the finance minister who presents the budget in the Lok Sabha. Atal argued, 'There is a patent anomaly arising from the appointment that the member who pilots the finance bills and appropriation bills will not be entitled to vote for it. As a natural corollary, the finance minister has always been a member from the Lok Sabha. This is so axiomatic that there is no dispute about this.' Pranab's job was saved because the speaker of the Lok Sabha struck down the argument.

However, at a personal level, Atal and Pranab shared a great equation and the two would, at times, go for walks together. They would also meet and have long discussions on various matters. Once, when the NDA government was in power, Pranab got into a row in the House about the practices of Hindu gods. When Murli Manohar Joshi challenged him, Pranab replied to him quoting Sanskrit shlokas with their English translations. Atal told Pranab, 'I warned Joshi not to take pangas with you on religious matters. He does not know that you have deep knowledge of the scriptures.'

The aide quoted earlier also says that Vajpayee never criticized anyone. He recollects the time when Anup Mishra, Atal's nephew, and the then BJP MP from Madhya Pradesh, came in with a BJP delegation to see the PM. 'You always say that Digvijaya Singh [the then chief minister of Madhya Pradesh] is a good man but he is troubling and harassing us,' said Mishra. Atal cut his nephew short and replied, 'Yes, I still say that he is a good man.'

The aide asserts that he never heard Atal raise his voice. He also adds that Atal always spoke in refined Hindi, even very angry. This is confirmed by retired IAS officer S.K. Das who says, 'We used to have frequent interactions with Atalji. But what struck me was that he never spoke ill of anyone. The only time I saw him take a jibe was at his political rival in those days, Balraj Madhok. Otherwise he was not at all judgmental and was very generous.'

He was also very informal and his position sat on his shoulders very lightly. 'In 1978, when he was the external affairs minister, one day we received a call from Atalji on our landline. He was looking for my mother whom he knew well. But what struck me is that he called directly without the assistance of personal assistants. This was quite against the mores of status conscious Delhi,' points out Sunita Budhiraja.

His former aide says that Atalji was a very private person and, given a chance, would spend all his time with his family. Contrary to his public image, he was a reserved person. Yet, he also had a wide range of friends and acquaintances. They would often drop by to meet him. 'This made it difficult for us to find a window to get files cleared. It was this huge circle of friends and contacts that he had which helped him to forge a consensus and made him acceptable to a wide range of people.'

Poets, not surprisingly, held a special place for Atal and would get immediate appointments. 'Once I went to meet him without a appointment but was immediately ushered into the room. The minister Rajnath Singh was there transacting some official business.

But the three of us sat together and had a long chat,' says poet Surendra Sharma.

In the same vein, poet Rajiv Krishna Saxena has mentioned on his site that he was surprised to get an appointment to meet Atal in February 2003. At that time, Atal was the prime minister; and on that particular day, Russian President Vladimir Putin was in town. Saxena wanted to gift a copy of his book to Atal and the prime minister spent a good fifteen minutes with him in spite of his busy schedule.

Shakti Sinha also says that Atal would give appointments easily and would meet people he knew even if they turned up without appointments. '"Now what to do, they have taken the trouble to come. I should meet them," Atal would remark,' says Sinha.

Shiv Kumar Kaul, an expert on tribal affairs, who had decades-long family ties with Atal, says, 'For long he used to call me "Guruji". When I went to meet him first after he became PM, he still called me Guruji and that also in public. This embarrassed me no end, but Atalji was not concerned.' Kaul also commends Atal for forming a separate ministry of tribal affairs. 'So many PMs were there before him but nobody had bothered to focus their attention on these long neglected tribes,' Kaul points out.

Atal was, however, himself called 'Guruji' by Chandra Shekhar, who was also the prime minister of India, albeit briefly. When Atal was speaking on a no-confidence motion moved by Chandra Shekhar after the demolition of the Babri Masjid, he was being heckled by Congress members. At this point Chandra Shekhar stepped in to bail him out.

Atal remarked, 'I am grateful to my honourable friend, Shri Chandra Shekhar. He has tried to assist his guru. It has always been a tradition that the guru, the teacher, should assist his disciple. But now such a time has come when the disciple has to come to the rescue of his guru.' To this, Chandra Shekhar responded, 'I will not be able to help you anymore.'

Incidentally, even in his student days, Atal was seen as a guru by his friends and companions. This was perhaps because he exuded the air of a man of wisdom. In fact 'Atal Guru' was his nickname during college days. In those days, the young man would sit at Godhaji hotel in Maharajwada area of Gwalior along with his friends, gossiping and discussing politics. Budding poets would also be part of the group. Atal would hold forth while other students listened with rapt attention.

Once Atal held forth on what was 'greatness'. He is believed to have said, 'Just to say that only the one who has won a victory is a great man is erroneous. If this were so then Rana Pratap and Prithviraj Chauhan would never have been considered great. Greatness does not come from bigness of position or out of victory in wars. Greatness comes out of showing respect for others and being sensitive to their needs.' Atal's co-students, who were mighty impressed with him, averred that one day he would become a great professor or a revolutionary poet.

As prime minister, Atal allowed his ministers a lot of latitude in their work. K. Padmanabhaiah, former home secretary to the Government of India, who was leading the Naga peace talks during the Vajpayee tenure, says, 'He only gave broad directions and allowed the ministers to deal with the nitty gritty. He was not a micro manager.' 'In meetings, Atalji would not allow any subject to linger on for long. If there was a controversy on a subject, he would ask the minister concerned to deal with it and move to the next matter,' he adds.

Atal's former aide concurs, 'Yes, he was known to take a broad view of things. Except for the time taken by us to find him free, getting a file cleared by him was not too difficult.' The aide reveals that it was only seldom that Atal refused to sign a file. 'Of course at that level the files would come vetted through many hands and all contentious issues would have been ironed out. But there are many top bosses who want to go through everything personally. However, Atalji was not in this category,' he adds.

'In meetings he would sometimes appear to be disinterested but would catch the essence,' says Padmanabhaiah, recollecting a meeting where Advani, Mishra and some others were also present. 'The conversation veered to Manipur and all of us were endlessly debating what had to be done. Mr Vajpayee appeared to doze off, but after some time intervened and pointed out that what we were discussing was the business of the Manipur government. "Why are we wasting our time on this matter?" he asked and shut all of us up.'

However, his apparent disinterest and monosyllabic answers sometimes confused those meeting with him. A former secretary of an important ministry, who was to head a team visiting the US for a negotiation, recollects a meeting to discuss what the negotiating stance should be and how much the delegation could yield. 'We presented the points that we wished to make in detail, and wanted directions. All through our presentation the prime minister had his eyes shut. Towards the end he opened his eyes and said: "Nahin hoyaga." We were at a loss because he did not clarify whether he was asking us to back off on some clauses or he was making a prediction.'

Shakti Sinha agrees, 'Boss was very attentive. He would absorb even minute details of what was was being said, though the impression that was conveyed was that he was not listening. He would process the information in his mind.'

Sinha also adds that Atal, like all successful politicians, was a good judge of people and knew how much to trust somebody. This ability stood him in good stead all through life. In fact, all his former aides refer to him as 'boss'.

At one level, Atal was an extremely well-informed PM. Atal's finance minister Yashwant Sinha has written in his memoirs about what happened after he called on J. Jayalalithaa, the then chief minister of Tamil Nadu. Apparently she gave him an envelope containing a letter about some of her tax cases. Sinha briefed Atal about the meeting but forgot to tell him about the envelope and the letter. After he finished talking and got up, Atal asked about the letter. In another instance, Yashwant Sinha had confided to Atal's principal secretary Brajesh Mishra and another official that he wanted to leave the finance ministry. Although Brajesh did not mention this to Atal, the latter came to know about the request because he called Yashwant Sinha and told him that he was doing a good job and there was no question of allowing him to exit the ministry.

Atal also read the newspapers very carefully; not surprising considering that he started his working life as a journalist. His aides remember that even as prime minister he would come to office after reading all the mainline English papers like the *Times of India* and *Hindustan Times* as well as the Hindi papers. In office, he would ask for important regional papers like the *Telegraph*. Eminent journalist Harish Khare recollected an incident in a recent edition (19 December 2014) of *Open* magazine. Khare said that he had run into Atal on 16 August 2001 at Parliament House. That morning, the *Hindu* had carried a piece by Khare about Atal's Independence Day speech from the ramparts of the Red Fort. Somewhere buried many paragraphs down in the story was the fact that Atal had read his speech from a written text. On seeing Khare, Atal asked, 'Why have you written that I read from a written text. On such occasions, one has to weigh one's words.' On checking with Brajesh Mishra, Khare understood that Atal was trying to tell him that, now that he was PM, he did not have the luxury of speaking extempore anymore.

However, whatever the case and whatever be the provocation, Atal was a nationalist who never compromised on national interest.

Journalist Bharti Sinha says, 'My father Indradeep Sinha was a CPI MP and a dyed-in-the-wool communist. But when I started to work on the BJP beat in late 1995, my father, who was totally opposed to the saffron party's philosophy, told me that Atal could be trusted for one thing, and that was national interest. He will never compromise national interest.'

Sinha says that subsequent events proved this. 'When there was pressure on the government to send troops abroad after the US started its war on terror, Atal realized this was against Indian national interest. Thus he took the matter to Parliament, where it was vetoed down,' the journalist points out. 'If he was really interested in sending troops, he would have taken an executive decision bypassing the Parliament.' Sinha also points out that before the matter reached Parliament, the left parties were trying to mobilize demonstrations against the move. However, the mobilization was not successful because of resource constraints. 'When Atal heard this from a senior left leader, he commented, "At least you should have told me this." You can guess what he meant,' says Sinha.

In a similar vein, eminent journalist Vinod Mehta wrote, 'I am convinced if Vajpayee had not been the PM, India would have been sent to fight in George Bush's Iraq invasion. He dreaded phone calls from George imploring him to send even a token force. "His soldiers are dying and now he wants my soldiers to die. I will never let that happen,"' Mehta remembered Atal having told him.

Mehta added that Atal summoned A.B. Bardhan and Harkishan Singh Surjeet (leaders from the left whose parties were holding demonstrations against the Iraq invasion) and asked them how the demonstrations were doing. They said that they were going well. Vinod Mehta further writes, 'Vajpayee said, "But I cannot hear anything." The canny old fox was suggesting that they raise the decibel level of the protests so he could tell Bush that his hands were tied. Note the subtlety of his strategy,' he adds.

Those who know him say that Atal is first to compliment people and is never shy of doing so. However, at the same time, he will never allow people to take advantage of their closeness to him. Once, on the occasion of Rakhi, Atal met one of his sisters who started asking him for various favours. Atal cut her short, saying, 'I am visiting you for Rakhi. Let's restrict the meeting to that purpose.'

Padmanabhaiah says that one year he was surprised and elated when he went to meet Atal to wish him on his birthday. The civil servant was accompanied by the director of the IB. The prime minister after accepting their birthday wishes, said, 'You two are able to save three hundred to four hundred lives in Nagaland every year due to your interventions. Thanks are due to you.'

The late ex-president A.P.J. Abdul Kalam recollected, at a public function many years later, how Atal embraced him in 1980 at a meeting organized by the then prime minister Indira Gandhi after the Indian Space Research Organisation (ISRO) had successfully launched SLV-3 which put the satellite Rohini into orbit. Atal was then an opposition leader and Kalam merely a defence scientist.

At the same time, when, on one of his visits, Padmanabhaiah recommended a Bharat Ratna for Pandit Bhimsen Joshi, Atal said, 'For Bharat Ratna no recommendations are accepted.' Padmanabhaiah persisted and said, 'He is getting old and may not live much longer.' Atal shot back, 'About twenty days back I attended his concert in Pune. He is fine.' There ended the conversation.

Even though he had a high stature and could afford to take things for granted, he never did so. Former ambassador Amit Dasgupta remembers how, in Brussels, all the MPs, who had come in an official delegation led by the speaker of the Lok Sabha in the early 1990s, raised a shindy when they were given single rooms instead of suites that had been proposed earlier. Atal was the exception; he readily accepted what was on offer. As Brajesh Mishra recollected in a television interview in 2009, many years after Atal had relinquished his position, 'He is by nature very liberal and generous in his thoughts. You criticize him today and tomorrow if the man who had criticized him asks for a meeting, he will say, ok come and talk to me. Now there are very few people who can do that.'

Atal is a fine example of a man who went places because of his public oration skills. He was still a journalist (though also a member of the RSS) when he had to stand in for Shyama Prasad Mukherjee at a public function in Gorakhpur in 1951. Since his train was delayed, Mukherjee could not reach on time although the audience had already gathered. In these circumstances, Atal had to keep the audience engaged and, hearing his speech, many important RSS functionaries like Nanaji Deshmukh proposed to Deen Dayal Upadhyaya that he be deputed to the Jana Sangh.

In Parliament, Atal impressed many with his oratory, which combined both thoughtful content and style of delivery. It is not that he was inhibited in his earlier years and gained confidence with time. Quite early on in his career, he had occasion to disagree with Pandit Nehru. He said on the floor of the Lok Sabha, 'I know that Panditji practices shirshasana and is welcome to continue doing so, but this does not mean that he should look at issues with an inverted vision.'

Sometimes he would come up with memorable quips. An old diplomat remembers that once, when on a visit to Lenin's mausoleum in Moscow to lay a wreath, Atal remarked, 'You know what is the difference between us and the Russians? In India *hum Shiv ki pooja karten hain aur yahan Shav ki.*'

Former diplomat and minister, Mani Shankar Aiyar (writing for NDTV.com on 27 March 2015) remembers Atal as a foreign minister visiting Islamabad and speaking in chaste Urdu at the official banquet. This was much to the chagrin of the Pakistani foreign minister, the Madras-born Aga Shahi, who knew very little

Urdu. Mani Shankar wrote, 'Atal spoke impeccable Hindi, almost never using an English word.' He added, 'His style of delivery was peculiarly his own, jocular but with rapier thrusts—never offensive but always telling.'

The former minister also recollected how, on the occasion of the fiftieth anniversary of the formation of the Lok Sabha in 2002, Atal bemoaned the state of affairs in Parliament, noting that how in the past MPs would walk out of the House to show their opposition but now they walked into the well of the House.

His aides say that Atal would speak better when the audience was large. 'In fact the larger the audience, the better would be the speech; audience *ka size dekh kar unko josh aa jaata tha*,' chuckles a former aide of his. 'He would give a different speech when he had a crowd of ten thousand and an entirely different one if there were a lakh people in front of him.'

The chief minister of Andhra Pradesh, Chandrababu Naidu, who is said to have had great leverage with the NDA government and Atal himself, says, 'He was a not a prime minister who would get into nuts and bolts. He used to seek and get a lot of advice from me.' Naidu claims to have influenced Atal on many policies, including a liberalized telecom policy and the ambitious programme to build highways. Atal always used to address Naidu as 'Babu' which was his popular nickname.

His friend of over fifty years, N.M. Ghatate, related a story that gives deep insight into Atal's personality, to the newspaper *DNA*, the day Atal was awarded the Bharat Ratna on 25 December 2014. The story relates to a national executive meeting of the BJP in Odisha (earlier Orissa) in its early days when the party did not have much of a following in the state. On the morning of the meeting Atal along with Ghatate went to the hall where the deliberations were to take place. When he found that the hall was not yet ready, Atal took the broom and began sweeping the floor himself. Seeing him wielding the broom, other workers followed suit. Atal continued sweeping till the floor had been cleaned and the carpets had been laid. As a minister in the Morarji government who espoused high principles, Atal used to believe in going by the rules and never misusing his official position. Old timers remember when he went to Gwalior as external affairs minister, on a weekend, he refused to sit in the official car provided by the district administration. Instead, he went in a Fiat car of a party associate. At the circuit house, Atal asked the large posse of policemen, 'It is the weekend and don't you have families that you are wasting your time here?' and sent them packing.

Another interesting incident took place in Gwalior when Atal went to visit the city after he first became an MP in 1957. He was invited to speak to the students of his college on the future of the youth. Atal spoke in a lighter vein and had the audience in splits; but in the course of the talk, he subtly delivered a tough message to the students, pointing out the three-point student formula. In the initial months students would take up a campaign for 'No Fees'. A few months later this would become 'No Attendance Requirement' and what remained, Atal quipped was a campaign for 'No Examinations'.

A senior leader of the BJP, who does not want to be named, says that even if Atal did not want to answer your question, he would ward off the query in a polite way so that the person who asked the question did not feel offended. He says, 'It was well-known that Atalji wanted Modi to resign after the 2002 riots and that, on a private flight to Goa, he was persuaded to change his mind. Later, I asked Atalji what transpired on the flight. He said, "*Pucho maat pucho maat kya kya nahin hua*," and skillfully deflected my question.'

Former economic convener of the BJP, Jagdish Shettigar, says, 'When party representatives like me went to him with problems, he would attentively listen to us nodding suitably. The same cannot be said about many other top leaders. With many of them you got the feeling that they were not even listening to you.'

A piece by Vinod Mehta sums up Atal's pleasant style. He wrote: 'It was impossible not to like him. Periodically I would go to 7 Race Course Road to have tea in his genial company. We would *gup-shup*. I told him the latest joke doing the rounds and he would pass on whatever came his way. He is the only PM I have known who has a sense of humour and enjoyed the exchange of witticisms. Once when I went to see him, he did not seem his usual jovial self. I asked him why he was so glum. He said, "*Apke baad Jayalalithaa aayengi.*" Then he laughed uproariously.'

His wit was evident even in the darkest of times. Once, during the Emergency, when Atal was released on parole, he went home to Gwalior. The entire neighbourhood, including children, had collected to see him. Atal asked a boy which school he studied in. The child innocently said, 'Saraswati Sangh'. On hearing this, Atal remarked with a straight face, 'Oh, your school bears the name Sangh. So hasn't Indira Gandhi banned the school?' This was an allusion to the ban on the RSS during the Emergency.

In spite of his powerful intellect, Atal, however, always had difficulty remembering names. An aide recollects that Atal would often say, '*Unhone jo patra likha, usko laao to* [Bring that letter that he has written].' This would throw the aides into a tizzy because they would have to figure out themselves which letter, written by whom, he was referring to. 'But gradually working with him, we could figure out what he meant. Because the clue to the letter he would be referring to would be in the subject that he was discussing,' the aide said, adding that working with him was a great learning experience.

SIX

Janata Raj and the BJP

WHEN THE JANATA GOVERNMENT came to power, Atal Bihari Vajpayee was appointed external affairs minister. This was natural because India's relationship with other countries had been a subject of great interest to Atal ever since he entered the portals of Parliament in 1957. On 26 March 1977, when Atal went to his ministerial office after taking oath in the Morarji Desai government, he instinctively realized that something was missing in the room. He had been there many times before as an MP and thus had a fairly good idea about what was there in the room. He soon spotted a vacant space on the wall and it immediately occurred to him that what was missing was a portrait of Jawaharlal Nehru that used to hang on the wall.

'This is where Panditji's portrait used to be,' he told his secretary, according to contemporary historian Ramachandra Guha (writing in the *Hindu* on 10 November 2002). 'I remember it from my earlier visits to the room. Where is it? I want it back,' he added. Guha attributes the information to a senior Foreign Service officer, still serving then.

Needless to add, the photo was soon fetched from the attic.

Atal knew that the rather clumsy spring cleaning was the effort of the babus to ingratiate themselves with the new regime by removing all signs of the old. However, Atal greatly respected Nehru, who held the external affairs portfolio in addition to being prime minister for all the seventeen years that he was at the helm. In fact, the external affairs minister's room was once used by Nehru when he was prime minister. After entering the room and asking his secretary about the missing photograph, Atal also asked that the window of the room be opened so that he could have a view of the North Block from there. When the window was opened, Atal remarked, '*Kabhi khwaabon mein bhi nahin socha tha ki ek din main is kamre mein baithunga* [Never did I dream that one day I will be sitting in this room].'

'He had watched Nehru with great admiration ever since he entered Parliament and had been greatly influenced by him, especially on foreign policy,' says veteran journalist Saeed Naqvi.

Little wonder then that under Atal, the Janata government's foreign policy did not show much change. In its hurriedly drafted manifesto, in the run up to elections, the Janata party had been rather vague on foreign policy. It had merely stated that the 'Janata Party's foreign policy will reflect the nation's enlightened interests and its aspirations and priorities at home. It will oppose all forms of colonialism and racism. It stands for friendships for all.'

At an election rally, Morarji Desai had promised that his government 'will make foreign policy reflect true non-alignment'. By this he implied that India's special relationship with the Soviet Union would be reviewed.

Once in the saddle, Atal realized that it was not possible to change the tilt that characterized India's foreign policy because there were compulsions which made the country's foreign policy what it was. If India was close to the USSR, it was because that country was a key supplier of arms, including sophisticated military hardware, to

India. Moreover, the USSR was a key partner in India's economic and industrial growth. Atal convinced Morarji about the strategic aspect of the relations between the two countries. This implied that if there had to be any change, there had to be continuity as well. Thus, while continuing good relations with the Soviet Union, Atal started pursuing the US too. As a result, US President Jimmy Carter came visiting India in 1978.

Atal had a proactive approach as the foreign office boss and touched base with neighbouring countries such as China and Pakistan. He realized that the quest for peace and good relations began from the neighbourhood. So China and Pakistan, with whom India had gone to war, would have to be tackled first. Atal visited China in February 1979, in what was termed as a significant visit, although the Chinese, always acting as the big brother, administered a bitter pill to India. While Atal was in Beijing, Deng Xiao Ping sent his army across to invade Vietnam. This was sacrilege because India shared a close relationship with Vietnam. To add insult to injury, Deng proclaimed that the invasion was meant to administer a lesson to Vietnam in the same manner as India had been taught one in 1962. Atal who was in the fifth day of his visit in Hangchow, immediately called off the trip and India condemned the aggression. However, Atal's attempt to normalize Sino-Indian relations was heralded as significant; coming as it did just two years after ambassadors had begun to be exchanged between the two countries, a practice that had ceased in the aftermath of the 1962 conflict. The trip was undertaken by Atal in response to an invitation from the Chinese foreign minister and had been originally slated for October/November 1978, but had been postponed since Atal was indisposed.

When, in the next general elections in 1980, Atal sought re-election from the New Delhi seat, he found his voters a trifle unhappy with him. They complained that he was never to be seen in his constituency. Atal himself apologized at public meetings. He said, 'People say I am always abroad. I cannot deny that charge but please give me another chance.'

Atal visited several countries during his tenure at the external affairs ministry. Other than China this included Afghanistan, Iran, Romania and the Soviet Union. Atal's trip to the United Nations general assembly is much remembered because he spoke in Hindi at the world forum. However, his message was not exceptional. He made a plea for a better world through harnessing modern science and technology, and appealed to the world community for universal peace based on freedom and justice. Making special reference to the problems in Africa, he ended his speech hailing, 'Jai Jagat [Victory to the World].' During a trip to the Soviet Union, Atal made it a point to emphasize to the leaders there that 'normalization of relations with other countries will not be allowed to affect relations with you'.

As a member of the erstwhile Jana Sangh, Atal was highly critical of Indira's West Asia policy and, therefore, with his becoming foreign minister, a review of this policy and closer ties with Israel were expected. In fact, the Israeli foreign minister, Moshe Dayan, made a secret visit to India in August 1977. However, the Israelis could not make much headway because Morarji Desai said no to ties with the Israelis till they withdrew from occupied Arab lands. Much to the surprise of the Americans and the Israelis, Atal himself said, 'There is no change in India's stand, Israel must vacate all occupied Arab territories and the legitimate rights of the Palestine people must be restored.'

Atal would have left a deeper mark on the foreign ministry if only the Morarji government had not begun tottering. Though the excesses of the Emergency had caused the opposition parties to make common cause and come together, they remained suspicious of each other. The Janata Party was riven by internal dissensions and soon there were factions in the party. The erstwhile socialists in the party were very suspicious of the erstwhile members of the Jana Sangh. Since there were 93 erstwhile Jana Sangh MPs in the Janata Party's total strength of 295 MPs, the socialists and others apprehended that the former would push their ideology and dominate the party. The socialists raised the issue of dual membership of such former Jana Sangh members, as they were members of not only the Janata Party but also of the RSS. The socialists demanded that the former Jana Sangh members relinquish their association with the RSS. However, Atal and his men would have none of this. They had all been connected with the RSS since their youth and there was no question of cutting off these ties.

A lot of the trouble had to do with the personal ambitions of Charan Singh who wanted to become prime minister at any cost. He was over seventy-five-years old and did not think that he would live for many more years. He was an old Congressman like Morarji and had taken part in the freedom struggle. The two had one thing in common: both had massive egos and were rigid. Charan Singh who, in the mid-1950s, had opposed Nehru's views on farm policies in an open Congress meeting, naturally started airing views about Morarji's economic policies. He was also critical of his government for not jailing Indira Gandhi for excesses of the Emergency. Later, as home minister, Charan Singh did arrest Indira Gandhi, only for the matter to end in a fiasco. Things soon came to a head and Raj Narain, who had defeated Indira Gandhi from the Rae Bareli constituency, broke away from the Janata Party and formed a parallel party with forty-nine MPs. This reduced the Janata Party to a minority and when the Congress leader Y.B. Chavan gave notice for a vote of no confidence, Prime Minister Morarji Desai resigned on 15 July 1979 before the vote was put through.

When Chavan was invited to form the government, he declined; but soon, in a bizarre development, Charan Singh staked claim to form the government. This claim was based on the support that he had from Indira Gandhi's party! Thus Charan Singh became prime minister; but before he could win a vote of confidence, the Congress party withdrew its support. Charan Singh was allowed to continue as caretaker prime minister for six months before elections were held again. Interestingly, when Charan Singh resigned, the Janata Party, which was still the single largest party, staked its claim. This time the leader was Jagjivan Ram who had defected from the Congress just before the 1977 elections. Atal was keen that the Janata experiment not fail and tried to help Jagjivan Ram cobble together a majority. He, in fact, was instrumental in liaising with M.G. Ramachandran of the All India Anna Dravida Munnetra Kazhagam (AIADMK) in getting the support of their seventeen MPs for the proposed Jagjivan Ram government. In the event, the government could not be formed because President Neelam Sanjiva Reddy, in a questionable move, dissolved the House without giving Jagjivan Ram any time.

The public had by then become thoroughly disillusioned with the Janata Party, whose constituents were cleaning their dirty linen in public. They gave Indira Gandhi, who had been ousted less than three years ago, the thumbs up and decidedly rejected the Janata Party, whose tally went down to thirty-one. Erstwhile Jana Sangh members made up seventeen of these thirty-one MPs. Atal himself could barely get himself re-elected to the Lok Sabha, winning by just 5,000 votes from New Delhi. His rival was a low-profile C.M. Stephen, who secured approximately 89,000 votes against Atal's 94,000. 'It was an absolute vote of no confidence against the Janata Party,' says former union minister Jaipal Reddy.

Atal, though a bit unpopular in his constituency because of his prolonged absence, had a high stature because of his visibility in the press. He was appreciated for the good work he had done as external affairs minister. 'Thus his small margin came as a surprise especially as the erstwhile Jana Sangh cadres were strong in the constituency,' says a retired government official who lived in Sarojini Nagar, a middle class government colony falling in the constituency.

The drubbing of the Janata Party did not end its woes. In fact, more was on the way. Soon after coming to power in New Delhi, Indira Gandhi had dismissed state governments which had been voted to power in 1977. Naturally, all of them were Janata led. With a fresh round of elections at hand, there was again tension in the ranks of the party. Once again, the issue of dual membership of erstwhile Jana Sangh members came to the fore. Atal believed that the RSS membership was just a ruse; the real fear was that the more disciplined Jana Sangh members, who originally came from a cadre-based party, would be able to dominate the proceedings in the party. Atal thought this was a misapprehension and he, along with his colleagues, had been trying to dispel it ever since the party was formed. However, it was to no avail. In the end it was decided that the members of the erstwhile Jana Sangh would go their own way.

On 5 and 6 April 1980, the erstwhile members of the Jana Sangh met at New Delhi's Feroz Shah Kotla and formed a new party headed by Atal Bihari Vajpayee. There was discussion whether the party should revert to its old name and be called the Bharatiya Jana Sangh once again. Vijaya Raje Scindia felt that it should be so. Atal, however, was of the opinion that the Jana Sangh was perceived as too hardline a party and it would be best if the new party was projected with a different image. Atal's and L.K. Advani's experience of working with the Janata government prime minister Morarji Desai had been good. Advani had served as the information and broadcasting minister in the Morarji government. The duo found that they were on the same page as Morarji, who was a Gandhian. Atal, along with Advani, had also been greatly influenced by Jayaprakash Narayan. Thus, Atal proposed that the new party should loosely model itself on the Janata Party; hence, the new outfit was to be called the Bharatiya Janata Party. Gandhian socialism was its credo and the flag of the party was adopted in good measure from the Janata Party.

Later that year, at the first public session of the party in Mumbai (earlier Bombay), Atal, who had been formally elected the president of the party, declared, '*Jayaprakash Narayan ke sapnon ko tootney nahin denge.*' He went on to add that Jayaprakash Narayan was not the name of a man, but a name that signified values and sincerity of values. He further said that the new party would resolve to finish Jayaprakash Narayan's work. For the BJP, politics would not become the game of the chair and it would not practise the politics of confrontation. The party would favour neither capitalism nor communism because both led to centralization. 'Vajpayee was a converted liberal. He realized that the public would accept the party more if it pursued a middle-of-the-road course,' says former union minister, Jaipal Reddy.

The Jana Sangh was seen as a right-wing Hindu party. To give the new party a more liberal image, the ranks of the party were opened to others as well and not merely confined to members of the erstwhile Jana Sangh. As a result, Sikander Bakht, a Muslim who had been the works and rehabilitation minister in the Morarji government and came from the Congress (O), was inducted into the BJP. Many others like Justice K.S. Hedge, a retired judge of the Supreme Court with no RSS background, also joined the party. In the elections to various states in mid-1980, the newly formed party, at the instance of Atal, adopted the manifesto of the Janata Party as its own manifesto. The party said that it stood for positive secularism which it defined as '*sarva dharma sambhava*'.

The RSS, however, was not very happy with the liberal turn taken by the new party. The RSS bosses, led by Balasaheb Deoras, had no problem with the party being called the Bharatiya Janata Party, but they did have problems with a party professing Gandhian socialism. Socialism was close to communism, an ideology that the RSS abhorred. Things came to a head the next year, in 1981, when an entire village of dalits in Meenakshipuram in southern Tamil Nadu got converted to Islam. The RSS was perturbed and decided to press into action a little-known cultural organization that had been lying dormant ever since it was founded in 1964. This was the VHP. The RSS began to increasingly use the VHP for Hindu mobilization after this incident. Meanwhile, the government under Indira Gandhi was becoming increasingly Hindu in its symbolism. Indira Gandhi began to visit temples visibly and tried to quell the Khalistan movement in Punjab with a strong hand. This gladdened the hearts of the RSS bosses who had always propagated a strong line against anti-national forces. For keen observers, the RSS was now clearly on the same page as the Congress, while the fledgling BJP was tottering even before it could firmly establish itself.

With elections approaching, Atal realized that although Indira's term was marked by troubles in Assam and Punjab and many scandals, it was only a combined opposition that could take on the ruling party. Therefore, he mooted the idea of a National Democratic Alliance (NDA) and began talking to various parties. Some were lukewarm in their approach and others were cold. The party that reacted positively was the Indian National Lok Dal (INLD) led by Charan Singh. Even though the earlier experience with Charan Singh had not been good, Atal was game for an alliance.

In party meetings, Atal called upon members to energize themselves and lambasted Indira. This was because Atal felt that the party was becoming complacent because it perceived that the Congress was not doing well after it lost assembly elections in Andhra Pradesh and Karnataka. Atal pointed out, at the national council meeting of the party in April 1983 at Delhi, that this complacency was the reason why the BJP had been routed in elections to the Municipal Corporation of Delhi and the Delhi Metropolitan Corporation. The defeat was a big shock to the BJP because this was the city where the party had begun from in its Jana Sangh days. An alarmed Atal resigned from the post of president of the BJP, but was persuaded to withdraw his resignation. In fact, Atal was also cajoled to accept a second term after his first term ended sometime in mid-1983.

At the national executive meeting of the BJP at Pune on 12 October 1984, just a few weeks before the assassination of Indira Gandhi, Atal declared, 'Our hour of trial is approaching. This government is a danger to democracy. In its insatiable lust for power, one single family has jeopardized the unity of an entire nation. In Punjab there is neither peace nor settlement. In Assam there is lull before a storm; a terrible crisis in Assam can erupt now.'

He went on to say, 'Though four months have elapsed since army action in Punjab, all the facts have not been made public. Nobody knows how many people died [in the Golden Temple]. How many were jawans, how many were terrorists and how many were innocent pilgrims? A Congress secretary says seven hundred jawans were killed but the government white paper gives a far less number.'

Atal also wondered whether Indira Gandhi was mulling a presidential system for India and was planning to rule India with the army sharing power. He said, '[The] PM is glibly telling the world that there is no harm in having a national debate on the desirability of the presidential system. One wonders if the PM has any clear concept apart from perpetuating her family in power.'

Atal also talked about politicization of the army. He pointed out that 'there was no martial law declared in Punjab yet senior officers, without relinquishing the commands in the army, are being appointed security advisors to the governor holding power and responsibility'.

The assassination of Indira Gandhi, on the last day of October 1984, just ahead of the general elections, had a cataclysmic effect. It is common wisdom that the RSS worked for the Congress party in the December 1984 elections. Whatever be the case, the Congress won 414 of 545 seats in the Lok Sabha, its biggest ever win that has never been bettered. The BJP was routed as it could merely win two seats. Atal Bihari Vajpayee also lost. The BJP merely got around 7 per cent of the votes against the Congress's 49 per cent. Reading the writing on the wall, Atal had decided to abandon New Delhi, the seat that he got elected from in 1977 and 1980.

Sympathy for the Congress, which had led to massive rioting in the aftermath of the assassination of Indira Gandhi, was palpable. There was no chance even for Atal and, in the worst-case scenario, he could lose his deposit as well. After confabulations with Vijaya Raje Scindia, Atal decided to return to Gwalior, his hometown. Vijaya Raje assured him safe passage. She apparently spoke with her son Madhav Rao, extracting a promise that he would not work against Atal and would allow him to win. The mother told the son that he could have the neighbouring seat of Guna to contest the polls. Armed with this assurance, Atal filed his nomination; but Rajiv Gandhi got wind of the supposed arrangement. Rajiv insisted that Madhav Rao contest from Gwalior. It was now too late for Atal to shift his seat, although he realized that he stood little chance against the local prince. Atal was defeated by a huge margin, Madhav Rao winning more than 3,00,000 votes or 66 per cent of all the votes cast. Atal got over 1,00,000 votes or 28 per cent of the total votes. This was the third time Atal had lost an election in his thirty-one-year long electoral career. He had lost earlier in 1953 from Lucknow, and in 1962 from Balrampur.

With the party having been wiped out in the polls, the BJP

was facing existential crisis and Atal had a lot of answering to do. Though it was argued that the sympathy wave for Rajiv Gandhi was too strong for the BJP to make any dent, in the ultimate analysis, in an election what mattered were the results. There is nothing that succeeds like success and conversely nothing fails like failure. Now the leadership of Atal and the path of Gandhian socialism were being called into question in the innermost sanctums of the party. The RSS too was pushing for reforms in the policies of the party, and the bosses in Nagpur were keen that the VHP and RSS work in tandem to pursue an agenda of Hindu mobilization. Atal was perturbed but could do nothing. He had an RSS background, but realized that an extreme path of Hindu mobilization may not be able to push the party into power. In such a situation, it was only to be expected that Atal would be pushed out of presidency of the party. This was done after an elaborate exercise which included an official committee set up under the aegis of a senior vice president of the party. Atal himself posed two questions to this official committee. He asked it to explore whether the 'party's defeat was because of our decision to merge the Jana Sangh with [the] Janata Party in 1977 and withdraw in 1980?'

The committee reported that both decisions were right but there was a communication gap between the leadership and grassroots workers, and the latter were not trained in ideology. Moreover, the party had failed to organize any popular movement since it was formed. In other words, the committee severely indicted Atal's leadership, without saying so directly.

The new man selected to lead the party was none other than Atal's close associate for nearly three decades, L.K. Advani. At its plenary session in New Delhi's I.P. Stadium, symbolically renamed Ekatmata Nagar in May 1986, Advani took over the reins with a clear directive from Nagpur to energize the party and build it up with cultural nationalism as its USP. Atal was out in the cold.

However, it was not entirely so; both the party and the bosses in Nagpur knew that Atal was an invaluable asset who could not be wasted. Not only was he a great orator but he also had tremendous stature. Thus, Atal was nominated for the Rajya Sabha from Madhya Pradesh. He took oath as an MP on 30 June 1986.

SEVEN

Witness to Ayodhya

SOME SENIOR POLITICAL LEADERS, who were in important positions during the late 1980s, claim that overtures were made to Atal Bihari Vajpayee to quit the BJP and join the fledgling Janata Dal at that time. Along with Atal, another BJP stalwart Bhairon Singh Shekhawat was also similarly approached. The duo were told that they would have no long-term future in the BJP because it was abandoning its original Gandhian philosophy and was being converted into a party with a Hindu ideology. Thus it would make more sense for them to join the Janata Dal, which would be a party like the Janata Party, on whose principles Atal had sought to construct the BJP.

These leaders say that both Atal and Shekhawat wavered for a moment, but ultimately spurned the overtures. They were steeped in the RSS culture and, therefore, could not think of abandoning their alma mater.

'We also did not persist with our efforts, not that it would have made a substantial difference, because the priority that V.P. Singh and we had was to break the Congress on the issue of corruption and not target the BJP and its Hindu agenda,' says a senior leader who was part of the effort.

V.P. Singh claimed in his memoirs, titled *Manzil Se Zyada Safar*, released in 2006 that Atal and Shekhawat wanted to break away from the BJP. Immediately after the release, Atal reacted strongly to the allegation and, in a written statement, said that V.P. Singh's claims were totally wrong. He said, 'The statement that I was unhappy with the party is not only far from the truth, it is also laughable.' Atal said that Singh's statements 'would lead to [a] wrong impression, so this statement is to remove doubts'.

In many interviews, when Atal was asked if he ever thought of leaving the party, he would jocularly answer, '*Jaayein to jaayein kahan?*' If the questioner persisted, he would say that the BJP was the best and that is why he always answered, 'If I have to go, where will I go?'

The stories about Atal mulling the option of leaving the BJP may not have been true, but the fact was that Advani was now the helmsman and what he did immediately after taking charge was to appoint a new team of office-bearers and infuse new blood into the system. He also dovetailed the programme of the BJP with that of the VHP that had embarked on the path of Hindu mobilization through ekatmata yatras, which were designed to bring out the faith and devotion of the masses towards Bharat mata and Ganga mata. The RSS also chipped in with its own efforts; the organization having remained distant from the BJP in the Atal era was now in the thick of things with jan sampark abhiyans. Advani himself was often seen in public, addressing various concerns. What is significant is that his tone had become strident, almost reminiscent of the Jana Sangh era. Circumstances too helped Advani. The young but inexperienced Rajiv Gandhi, who had come to power in the elections that followed the assassination of his mother, started stumbling. The most well-known instance is the Shah Bano case, where used his party's brute majority in Parliament to push through a regressive legislation against the rights of Muslim women. The Supreme Court had ordered the husband of Shah Bano, who had been left with no means of livelihood when she was divorced after decades of marriage, to pay her maintenance. Orthodox Muslims rose against the order, citing Muslim Personal Law, and Rajiv Gandhi capitulated, much to the chagrin of the BJP, which got a chance to dub the Congress a pseudo-secularist party pandering to orthodox Muslims.

Things, however, begun heating up with the outbreak of the Bofors scandal. Powerful people, including Rajiv Gandhi, were suspected of having been paid kickbacks to the tune of ₹64 crore by a Swedish company called Bofors AG for the purchase of field guns by the army. This, in a way, acted as a signal for the Advani-led party to bring the Ram Janmabhoomi issue, that had been lying dormant, into focus. As per legend, Lord Rama was born at a place in Ayodhya and the temple that stood at his birthplace had been razed by the invading Mughal army of Babur. In its place, a mosque called the Babri Masjid had been erected in 1528. In 1949, shortly after independence, an idol of Ram lalla had mysteriously made its way inside the mosque. Following court orders, the mosque had been sealed but the idol was allowed to remain inside. Daily puja was done by a pujari who was allowed access twice a day. However, a fresh court order in February 1986 opened up the mosque doors. The VHP now began firming up plans for constructing a Ram temple at the site and even had a blueprint made of the proposed temple. At the same time, bricks were being consecrated at temples across the nation. They were slated to be carried to Ayodhya to be used for the construction of the temple. In June 1989, as elections approached and it became increasingly clear that the Congress would not be re-elected, the BJP brought up the Ram Janmabhoomi issue in the national executive.

So, was Atal sidelined when Adavni took over as president in those tumultuous times? 'I would not say so although that was the impression in the political circles,' says P. Shivshankar, an important Congressman who had served in the cabinets of both Indira and Rajiv Gandhi.

Shivshankar said that Atal and Advani had a symbiotic relationship which meant that the latter always consulted the former. 'Vajpayeeji was in the know of things and offered advice on various matters though he was not the helmsman,' the former minister says. Thus, Atal took a backseat even as Advani propelled the party forward. But Atal was always considered a more senior leader of the party by the public at large.

Anil Khanna, a young Delhi-based executive at that time, remembers, 'I clearly recollect the slogan "*Atal Advani kamal nishan maang raha hai Hindustan*" being raised by the BJP in the 1989 election campaign.'

Incidentally, writing in the *Indian Express* two decades later in December 2009, Advani said, 'He [Atalji] had reservations about the BJP getting directly associated with the Ayodhya movement. But he accepted the collective decision of the party showing that he was a thorough democrat by conviction and temperament.'

Whatever be the case, Atal did not contest the 1989 Lok Sabha polls. Though he was a Rajya Sabha MP, this was a little unusual because he always preferred membership of the Lok Sabha to a position in the Upper House. The Congress won 197 seats in the polls in which it was pitted against the National Front. The latter was a coalition of various parties, led by the Janata Dal of V.P. Singh, that had fought the elections in alliance with regional parties like the TDP, Dravida Munnetra Kazhagam (DMK) and Asom Gana Parishad (AGP). There were seat understandings with the left parties and BJP too. The grouping was to unite the anti-Congress votes. The tally of the Congress fell far short of a majority and thus was not enough to form a government. Since the Congress was the single largest party, President R. Venkataraman called upon Rajiv

Gandhi to form the government. He, however, declined and thus the invitation went to V.P. Singh, who had earlier been Rajiv Gandhi's finance and defence minister but had quit the government and the party protesting against corruption. The Janata Dal had won 143 seats and it required the support of the BJP (that had 85 seats) and the left parties to form the government. V.P. Singh invited both to join the government but both declined and instead promised to support it from outside. The BJP held that they had contested the elections on separate manifestos so it did not make sense for it to join the Janata Dal government. Additionally, the Janata experiment (not more than ten years old) was still fresh. The BJP did not want an encore of the dual membership issue.

The V.P. Singh government did not take much time to get into trouble. Although the former Congressman led a minority government, he wanted to push a radical political agenda. He pulled out a ten-year-old Mandal Commission report, that was gathering dust somewhere, and announced that he would implement its recommendations. The report had recommended that job reservations that were limited to scheduled castes and tribes be extended to other backward communities (OBCs) as well. V.P. Singh wanted to create a political base for himself amongst the OBCs, so that he would be unshakable. However, the public reaction was very adverse in urban centres. The BJP also saw in the move an attempt to counter its plans to consolidate the Hindu vote. Immediately, L.K. Advani took the decision to set out on a rath yatra to mobilize Hindu opinion. The objective of the yatra obviously was not to oppose OBC reservations but to mobilize Hindu opinion on the Ram Janmabhoomi issue. This would have the impact of unifying the Hindu vote. The rath yatra began on 25 September from Somnath on the west coast and was to reach Ayodhya on 30 October after traversing thousands of kilometres.

V.P. Singh had fired his Mandal missile on 7 August, but even before that the VHP was actively pursuing its Ram temple agenda. In November 1989, when Rajiv Gandhi was still at the helm of affairs, the VHP had symbolically laid the foundation stone for the temple at a site close to the Babri Masjid. The VHP also declared its intention to start construction work on 1 February 1990, and called upon the Muslims to voluntarily move the mosque to some other spot. By that time V.P. Singh was in power and, realizing that trouble could be at hand, he requested Atal to ask for more time, four months to be precise, from the VHP. Atal acceded and interceded on behalf of V.P. Singh, seeking more time from the VHP. Since the request had been conveyed through Atal, the VHP leadership agreed. After four months had elapsed and the VHP perceived that the government had done nothing to resolve the problem, it decided to start work on the temple on 30 October. This was the day on which Advani planned to reach Ayodhya at the end of his rath yatra.

In the end, however, Advani did not reach his destination. He was arrested in Bihar on 23 October by the Janata Dal-led state government of Lalu Prasad Yadav for endangering communal harmony. While the yatra was on, V.P. Singh had once again sought Atal's intervention to convince the VHP to start work for building the temple on an undisputed area. But this plea did not yield any result.

There was unprecedented crackdown in UP and Bihar, but pilgrims defied orders to reach Ayodhya where there were pitched battles between them and the police. Many died in police firing. There was rioting in many parts of the country. In the meanwhile, not unexpectedly, the BJP pulled the plug on the V.P. Singh government. As a result, the government fell on 10 November 1990, just eleven months after it came into being.

A few months and the short-lived government of Chandra Shekhar (who, incidentally, made earnest efforts to resolve the

Ayodhya problem) later, the country was back to another poll in the summer of 1991. This time the mood in BJP circles was distinctly upbeat. It was obvious that the party had collected many supporters owing to its own efforts and those of the VHP in the previous two years. Atal decided to contest the polls to the Lok Sabha and chose Lucknow, the capital of UP, to contest from. For Atal any seat was a sure-shot winning seat but Lucknow more so, because Ayodhya, where Hindu mobilization was at its the maximum, was not too far off from the city. Lucknow also happened to be the seat from which Atal had first contested elections in 1953, although he had lost on that occasion.

Atal won hands down, garnering almost 2,00,000 votes, which accounted for approximately 50 per cent of the votes polled in the constituency. His nearest rival from the Congress polled merely 20 per cent of all votes cast. The BJP won 120 seats, improving its tally from 85 seats in the previous election. The party also consolidated its vote base, from 11 per cent in 1989, to 20 per cent. Atal was no longer seen as occupying the backseat. Now public analysts began saying that Advani was the hardliner in the party with a Hindutva face and Atal was the moderate face of the BJP and that both had their respective roles to play.

Halfway through the election, Rajiv Gandhi was assassinated. This had the impact of the Congress winning more seats in the second phase of the polls, that took place after the assassination of Rajiv. The party won 232 seats even as the Janata Dal was reduced to a tally of 59. A Congress government headed by P.V. Narasimha Rao, who was in retirement mode before the elections and had not contested the polls, came into office.

A few months later, assembly elections were also held in UP and many other states. The BJP came to power in UP with voters influenced by the chants of 'Jai Shri Ram' opting for the saffron party. As a result, the party won 221 seats in a House of 425. This was even as the central leadership of the party, primarily Atal, was concerned that the party was seen as an outfit with a singular agenda, of building a temple. This was affecting the prospects of its expansion in areas where the Ram temple issue did not strike such a chord. Thus, the thinking was that the party should go a little slow on the Ram temple agenda. Around this time, Advani also had to step down from the post of president of the BJP because the party's constitution did not allow him more terms. The new president, Murli Manohar Joshi, was keen to leave a mark and took up Kashmir as an issue.

Trouble in Kashmir had become a big issue since 1989, and he embarked on an ekta yatra from Kanyakumari to Srinagar. But the VHP, finding that the circumstances were more favourable than ever before for the building of the Ram temple, with a BJP government ruling in UP, was not willing to miss the chance. It stepped up pressure on UP's Kalyan Singh government, to remove all legal and administrative hurdles to the building of the temple. Kalyan Singh was reluctant to begin with but announced that 18 November 1992 would be the day when kar seva would begin. Sensing the public mood, the BJP put its weight behind the campaign, with Advani and Murli Manohar Joshi touring the state of UP to motivate people to participate in the construction of the temple. Atal, however, kept a discreet distance from these activities. 'Vajpayeeji wanted the Ram temple but he wanted to be more careful about how this was done,' says Congressman Shivshankar.

By the end of November, thousands of people had collected in Ayodhya for kar seva that was slated for Gita Jayanti on 6 December. What happened on 6 December 1992 is well known. Crowds started collecting in huge numbers outside the Babri Masjid. They were belligerent and were straining at the barricades on all sides of the mosque. UP Chief Minister Kalyan Singh had sworn in an affidavit to the Allahabad High Court that the kar seva would be symbolic. Meanwhile, L.K. Advani and other BJP leaders, but not Atal, visited the site at around 11 a.m. However, they quickly exited the place. In the afternoon, some kar sevaks broke through the barricade and were followed by a delirious crowd. Within hours, the Babri Masjid had been razed to the ground.

Atal had not been to Ayodhya, but the previous day he was in Lucknow addressing kar sevaks at Jhandewalan Park in Aminabad. He was captured in a video, ostensibly recorded by the intelligence, which is freely available on YouTube. Writing in the Lucknow edition of *The Times of India* in the run up to the 2014 general elections, under a report titled 'Did Vajpayee have premonition about Babri Masjid demolition', journalist Ashish Tripathi quoted from the video where Atal is seen saying, 'The Supreme Court has allowed bhajan kirtan (at the appointed spot) which cannot be performed by one man. Many people have to be present for that. You can't sing kirtans sitting down. How long can one stand? Sharp stones are there on the ground—you can't sit on them either. The ground has to be leveled. I do not know what will happen there. I wanted to go to Ayodhya but I was told to go to Delhi.' He didn't clarify who had told him to go to Delhi.

Two decades later, the Liberhan Commission, enquiring into the demolition of the Babri Masjid, held twenty-eight persons responsible for the act. Atal's name also figures in the list. The commission labelled Atal, Advani and Murli Manohar Joshi, 'pseudo moderates'. The report held that Atal was 'pretending to keep a distance' from the Ram Janmabhoomi campaign, 'but he was actually part of the conspiracy'. The commission said in its report that the demolition of Babri Masjid was neither 'spontaneous nor unplanned'. The report also held that 'the attempts by the pseudo moderate elements within the parivar were predictably of little significance and were destined to fail, whether by design or otherwise'.

Interestingly, on 17 December 1992, in his first speech after the demolition of the Babri Masjid, Atal said in the Lok Sabha, 'I am sorry for the demolition of the structure. I usually come across people who are of the opinion that it has been a blot for 400 years and there was no alternative but to remove this blot. I am afraid of such sentiments.' He further added, 'I am unhappy about whatever happened in Ayodhya on 6 December. I am ready to go one step ahead and ask those kar sevaks, who were small in number, to come forward and openly confess that they have demolished the structure and for that they are ready to face the music. I think a group out of the mob emerged and they refused to follow the leaders and attacked and demolished the structure. It was very bad.'

On the subject of Advani's rath yatra, Atal said, 'When Shri Advani went on rath yatra, I had my reservations. I had earlier said that it would not serve any purpose. But the way people supported the cause and the mistakes that were made by the ruling party, the arbitrary decisions by the then Chief Minister Shri Mulayam Singh Yadav to deal with the agitation, the way communalism was incited by the announcement that a particular community had the right to have arms, worsened the situation.'

A few years later, on 6 December 2000, by when he had become prime minister, Atal was, however, speaking a different language. He said, 'Ram temple construction is an expression of national sentiment that is yet to be fulfilled. The entire country wants the temple. The Muslims do not oppose it.' He also said that on the fateful day of 6 December 1992, L.K. Advani, Murli Manohar Joshi and Uma Bharti were in Ayodhya 'to protect the Babri Masjid not demolish it'.

In its 18 December 2000 issue, *India Today* carried an article on the subject of Atal's statements that said sarcastically, 'One of the hallmarks of a successful politician is that he should mean all things to all men.'

This comment apart, Atal revealed his mind many years later in interviews. He said that in his opinion, the Ayodhya problem should have been settled at the local level in a fashion similar to the way the Somnath issue was sorted out after independence. The oceanfront temple of Lord Shiva on the Saurashtra coast had been destroyed by invaders many times in the medieval era. After independence, a national consensus was built and the temple was reconstructed. In Atal's opinion, a Ram temple should have been built in Ayodhya when the Ayodhya movement was at its peak. This alone would have ensured that the Babri Masjid was not demolished.

EIGHT

Post Ayodhya to Prime Minister

THE CULMINATION OF THE Ayodhya movement was a moment of glory for Advani. It seemed that he was now in an unassailable position and that the sidelined Atal had totally lost out. Many in the saffron party believed that it was a matter of time before the Narasimha Rao government fell and a government headed by Advani took office.

However, politics is unpredictable. So, surprisingly, the BJP was soon in a downslide. The first jolt that the party got was in UP a few months later when fresh assembly elections were held there, after the BJP government was dismissed in the aftermath of the demolition of the Babri Masjid and the assembly dissolved. The party, with 177 seats, had 44 seats less than its tally of 221 (in a House of 425) in the previous election in 1991. There was, however, a 2 per cent increase in the vote share from 31 per cent to 33 per cent. Political analysts perceived this is as evidence of a marginal increase in the support base of the party, but the lower number of seats meant that other parties had ganged together against the BJP. That is why even after recording a higher percentage of votes, the party got less seats. The major gainer of the election was the

Bahujan Samaj Party (BSP), a party advocating the dalit cause. Since the BJP under Advani had sought to include dalits in the Hindu cause of the temple, this implied that even if they had been swayed by the Ram Janmabhoomi issue, when it came to voting they had stood behind the BSP. Also, it was obvious that the ganging up of various parties, implicitly so, had happened because many no longer trusted the BJP and Advani after Ayodhya—more so as the demolition of the Babri Masjid brought in its wake bloody riots leading to nearly a thousand deaths in Mumbai, Surat, Bhopal and many other places. The Mumbai RDX bombings in March 1993, in reaction to Ayodhya, that led to the deaths of over three hundred people, also led to a fall in the BJP's equity, both nationally and internationally.

The party was now perceived as an outfit of rabble rousers and fire-breathing hardliners. What strengthened this image was the assertion made by elements in the Sangh Parivar that after the reclamation of the Ram Janmabhoomi they would now 'liberate' Kashi where a mosque stood next to the Vishwanath temple. The mosque had been constructed by Aurangzeb after destroying the temple. But two centuries later, the temple had been reconstructed, leaving the mosque intact. Now the hardline elements wanted to destroy the mosque and expand the temple. Additionally, they also wanted to reclaim the Krishna Janmabhoomi in Mathura.

In such circumstances, no other party was willing to do business with the BJP. This dealt a blow to the leadership of Advani (because he was seen as the patron of the extreme elements in the party), and this meant, conversely, that Atal, as the moderate face of the party, was more acceptable than him.

But what made Advani's continuance untenable was something else—the hawala scandal and the Jain diaries. It was alleged that many top Indian politicians, including L.K. Advani, had been paid bribes by businessmen in the period between 1987 and 1991. As proof of this, the diary of a businessman, S.K. Jain, was produced by law enforcement agencies. The politicians were from various parties. Following a public interest litigation in the Supreme Court, the Central Bureau of Investigation (CBI) investigated the case and chargesheeted many politicians, including L.K. Advani. Even before he could be chargesheeted, Advani, reading the writing on the wall, passed on the baton to Atal. He also vowed not to contest elections before he was absolved of the charges. The transfer of leadership took place at the party's annual meeting in 1995 in Mumbai. Without telling anyone or consulting the RSS, Advani stood up and told the audience that the BJP's prime ministerial candidate for the next general elections, slated in 1996, would be Atal Bihari Vajpayee. There was momentary silence in the hall before the audience broke into applause. Slogans of '*Agli baari Atal Bihari*' rent the air.

'Advaniji realized that it was not possible for him to continue and without any prompting passed on the mantle of leadership to Atalji', says Jagdish Shettigar, who was the convener of the economic cell of the party and a national executive member then. Shettigar adds, 'Advaniji understood that other parties would do business with the BJP only if it was headed by Atalji. And the BJP's support base was not broad or deep enough to propel it to power on its own.'

Thus, the Ayodhya movement (although it had resulted in the sidelining of Atal) ultimately worked to his advantage and brought him back centrestage.

In 1997, however, Advani was absolved of all allegations in the hawala scandal by the Delhi High Court. On 22 December 2014, nearly two decades later, television channel CNN IBN asked Advani why he had ceded position to Atal and announced him as the prime ministerial candidate in 1995. Advani said that Atal was the 'natural choice' and therefore his naming of Vajpayee could not be taken as an instance of his ceding ground. Advani said that Atal was his role model and guide all through their decades-old association. However, when asked how the two worked together in the period when Advani became important in the party in the late 1980s, he was evasive. He answered that the two worked together well and digressed, saying that Atal was well known for his culinary skills and made good khichdi! Clearly, there was some tension between the two, but party insiders say that Atal never passed any comments against Advani during this period, except once disapproving of Advani being weighed against blood donated. Another time, pointing to the rath yatris, he is said to have commented, 'Dekho dekho, there goes Advaniji's vanarsena.' A party insider says, 'Atalji was dignified and took everything in his stride.'

Many think that the hawala case against Advani was a stratagem by the Narasimha Rao regime to keep him away from centrestage. Narasimha Rao was perceived to be a soft Hindu and his associates felt that he apprehended that he could be upstaged by Advani. Hence, the hawala case was instituted. Rao had good relations with Atal and any day preferred him over Advani, say those in the know of things. However, there is no real evidence to suggest that the case was deliberately instituted by the Rao regime. Moreover, following a public interest litigation that had been filed, the Supreme Court had handed over the case to the CBI and was monitoring it. Thus, the apex court had more to do with the case than the government. However, the Rao government did put indirect pressure on the BJP and Advani when, in 1994, the then home minister S.B. Chavan sought to amend the Constitution to delink politics from religion and bring in a change in the Representation of People's Act to derecognize parties that did not conform to the basic tenets of secularism. This move was a thinly disguised attempt to put the BJP on the backfoot.

In the late 1980s and very early 1990s, Atal appeared morose to many who knew him reasonably well. But as the party grew, his optimism also returned. As the BJP's political stock grew, many important persons in the country, who were fed up with the Congress raj, began to flock to the party and its offices. Atal used to be a regular fixture at the BJP headquarters at 11, Ashok Road in New Delhi those days, and was busy meeting people. Many important people sought to meet Atal whom they were more comfortable with than Advani. At this time, the leader of the BJP parliamentary party was, however, Advani.

'Every morning top leaders of the party would meet together for informal discussions in the BJP office. Views would be exchanged on a wide range of matters,' says Shettigar.

One of the important persons with whom Atal would confabulate those days was Brajesh Mishra, who would later become his principal secretary and national security advisor. Even then party insiders knew that Atal was taking rigorous briefing on foreign affairs from Mishra. Many who joined the party in the early 1990s, found Atal open and welcoming. 'He was ready to listen to us and sought our point of view. He encouraged us to talk. I found him very endearing,' says a former civil servant who joined the party in 1991.

Some insiders think that Atal also gained because Murli Manohar Joshi was asserting himself as a leader as he had been the president of the party for two years. 'This meant that Advani had to contend with not only Atal but also Murli Manohar Joshi. The latter was also a hardliner, so his presence tended to challenge in some ways the leadership of Advani. The result was that it was advantageous for Atal.'

A lot of water has passed through the Ganga and Yamuna in the last twenty years and the country's politics has changed. But in the mid-1990s only a moderate leader like Atal was acceptable to the masses.

'If a moderate Atal were to be challenged by the hardcore Advani in contemporary times, the situation would have been different. The country has now moved into an era of intense right-wing politics which was not the case then,' says a party insider, who would rather not be identified.

Jyotirmaya Sharma, a Hindutva expert, is of a different opinion. He says it is all about occupying the 'middle ground' in politics. He avers that Atal understood that to be successful in politics in India one has to be on the 'middle ground'. This, according to Sharma, means that even if one has an extreme view on some subject, one can articulate it but not push it to the extremes. Atal knew this but Advani wore his heart on his sleeve and, at least in the mid-1990s, did not know how to retract himself from his position, says. Thus, Atal may have been interested in the Ram temple but was not seen as intractable, unlike Advani, says Sharma.

As election time came closer, it seemed clearer that Narasimha Rao would not be able to make the cut a second time. The Rao government had been surrounded by controversies from the beginning. There was the Jharkhand Mukti Morcha (JMM) scandal, wherein some MPs from the party had been bribed in exchange for their support to the minority government on the floor of the House in 1991. Then Harshad Mehta, the prime accused in the stock exchange scam of 1992, claimed that he had been to Narasimha Rao's house along with an industrialist and had personally paid ₹1 crore in cash. This payment was a donation to the Congress party but was naturally seen as quid-pro-quo for letting him off the hook. Numerous other scandals like the fertilizer scam and the sugar scam tainted the Narasimha Rao government. All this dented its image.

The main achievement of the regime was to initiate the process of liberalization in the economy and pull it out of a morass, by freeing industry from licensing and other controls. When Narasimha Rao took over, the foreign exchange position was so fragile that the country had to pawn its gold reserves (lying in the vaults of the

Reserve Bank of India [RBI]) to borrow from abroad. The initial efforts at reforms had been lauded by all. In fact, Atal and his party claimed in private that the agenda pursued by the Rao government was actually the programme set out by the BJP. However, faced with opposition from powerful lobbies, the process of reforms was halted in 1995, allowing Atal and his party to criticize the government that was already groaning under the burden of anti-incumbency.

By the time campaigning for the 1996 election began, Atal was sure that the BJP would come to power. Journalist Bharti Sinha says, 'I accompanied him as a journalist during his campaign. He got solid applause and crowd response wherever he went out to campaign,' Sinha, whose father was a Communist Party of India (CPI) MP says that even in her father's area in Bihar, that was in those days a communist stronghold, Atal got a huge response. 'This was quite apparent,' she says. Sinha also adds that Atal himself seemed quite confident, 'He turned to me at one point and said that, "looking from crowd response, it seems that *main pradhan mantri baan hi jaoonga*".'

Veteran political analysts recall that the 1996 elections were the first where the effects of the expenditure limits set by the Election Commission and its ban on loudspeakers began to be seen. In this lacklustre election, the BJP took a leaf out of the Congress's book and started projecting Atal Bihari Vajpayee as prime minister in waiting. In the past, the Congress had woven its election campaign around the persona of a member of the Nehru-Gandhi family. For the first time, the Congress candidate—Narasimha Rao—was not from the Nehru-Gandhi family. BJP strategists very smartly projected the electoral battle as an Atal versus Rao fight, instead of a BJP versus Congress one. '*Ek ek kar ke sabki baari, ab ki baari Atal Bihari,*' was the slogan raised by BJP cadres.

Since Rao was perceived as a weak leader and his government had been rocked by corruption, the strategy seemed to work.

The previous two elections of 1989 and 1991 had seen the party aggressively pursuing the Ram temple agenda. This time the BJP put it on the backburner except in UP, where it promised that the temple would soon be built. The party also campaigned on the slogan of '*Parivartan ke ore* [Towards change]' and bombarded voters with posters, pamphlets, banners and Atal badges. Films and advertisements were also released. Atal himself sought re-election from his Lucknow constituency. Since he was missing from his constituency (because he had to canvass all across the country), a sculptor was commissioned to prepare Atal's bust. This was paraded across the constituency so that the voters could at least see his bust if not the real him. BJP strategists felt that this was essential because his rival, cine star Raj Babbar, was campaigning vigorously across the length and breadth of the constituency. In the end, not surprisingly, Atal won the elections convincingly; polling about 4,00,000, or 52 per cent, of the votes. Raj Babbar, who contested on a Samajwadi Party ticket, secured about 3,00,000, or 36 per cent, of the votes cast. Amazingly, there were fifty-eight candidates in the fray. The candidate who came last polled a mere forty-one votes. However, the voting percentage in the constituency was pretty low at 51 per cent. It was surprising that even the presence of a prime ministerial candidate had not motivated the voters to turn out in larger numbers.

The BJP came out tops in the election, winning 161 seats. This was more than the 140 seats secured by the Congress. Strangely, however, it polled a lower percentage of votes (at 20 per cent) than the Congress (which polled 28 per cent of the votes). This meant that the Congress vote base was spread wider and that of the BJP was more concentrated, which allowed it to secure more seats with a lower percentage of votes. President Shankar Dayal Sharma called upon the leader of the BJP, that is Atal, to form the government. This was even though the party had won far less than the 272 halfway mark in the House of 543 MPs. Atal accepted the offer from the president and became the first BJP prime minister of the country on 16 May 1996.

However, at the end of thirteen days, Atal realized that he could not cobble together a majority, what with the left and the Congress joining forces to keep the BJP out of power. Only the Shiv Sena, Akali Dal and Samata Party had agreed to go with the BJP. Atal announced on the floor of the Lok Sabha that he would resign, and in a speech that was telecast nationally on Doordarshan, he made a strong plea. This was the first time that a political speech was being telecast on television to an audience across the country, which sat riveted before the television. Atal, in his poignant speech, harped on the politics of negativism and reactionary politics: 'That is politics to stop us at any cost by making untouchables of us—this is not healthy politics.'

He also argued that 'I have been accused that I am craving for power and my acts are as a result of my craving for power. If people have given my party the highest number of seats, should I shy away from staking a claim for power? Should I run away from the battlefield to betray the confidence reposed by the people in making us the single largest party?'

Atal also answered the charge that his party should not have tried to form the government since the BJP got only a minority of votes. He pointed out that the first-past-the-post Westminster system that was followed in the country counted only the seats that a party won and not the percentage of votes polled. By implication, the BJP could not be blamed for jumping in to try and form a government.

That day the BJP stood isolated and failed to hold on to the government, but Atal's powerful speech did not fail to stir a large number of people who watched him speak emotionally. This certainly had a positive impact on the prospects of the party in future polls, which was visible two years from then. For the record, Atal's thirteen-day government was succeeded by a broad left-of-centre alliance, led by the then Karnataka chief minister H.D. Deve Gowda, which took office in June 1996. The government lasted till the third week of April 1997 with tension between the coalition partners and the Congress, on whose support the government depended, pulling it down. Two days later, I.K. Gujral, who had, many years ago, been a close associate of Indira Gandhi's, came at the head of the same alliance. The government led by Gujral lasted a few months before falling.

There were fresh elections in March 1998 and the BJP again emerged as the party with the most number of MPs. It won 182 seats and polled 25 per cent of the votes cast, increasing both its tally of seats as well as votes polled. Atal himself had again contested from Lucknow and won by a massive majority, polling 57 per cent of the votes. In the contest involving fourteen candidates, at second place was Muzaffar Ali of the Samajwadi Party.

This time many other parties were willing to do business with the BJP. Besides its old allies, the TDP of Andhra Pradesh, the AIADMK of Tamil Nadu, and the Biju Janata Dal of Odisha joined the National Democratic Alliance government. The combination was basically an anti-Congress front because all the parties that joined were regional parties that had the Congress as their main opposition in their states. Thus, Atal Bihari Vajpayee again became the prime minister on 19 March 1998 with a thin majority. This government was to last for thirteen months.

The government this time fell after the AIADMK withdrew its support. AIADMK supremo Jayalalithaa had a whole range of demands that the Atal government was unable to fulfil. Among these was the dismissal of the DMK government that ruled Tamil Nadu. Jayalalithaa had been arraigned in a major corruption case and desperately wanted the state government out. She had supported the Atal government for this unstated reason.

After the AIADMK withdrew support, Atal and his allies made a herculean effort to rescue the government but, in a match down to the wire, it lost the no confidence motion in the Lok Sabha by just a single vote. On 17 April 1999, the government got 269 votes in its favour while 270 votes went against. On the morning of that day, Atal spoke to BSP chief Mayawati, who promised to support the government. However, when Mayawati stood up to address the Lok Sabha, she announced that her party would vote against the government. Saifuddin Soz of the National Conference defied his party bosses and went against the government, and Congressman Giridhar Gamang, who had not resigned his membership of the Lok Sabha in spite of being the chief minister of Odisha for the last few months, voted against the government.

Atal was heartbroken after the government fell and the scene was described by his advisor Sudheendra Kulkarni. Writing in the *India Today* thirty-fifth anniversary issue, in November 2011, Kulkarni disclosed, 'I remember how heartbroken Atalji was that day. After the vote, he emerged out of the Lok Sabha and walked ever so slowly to his office in room number ten of the Parliament House. As soon as he entered the room which was already filled with his senior colleagues, he broke down. "*Hum keval ek vote se haare, keval ek vote,*" he said, tears running down his face.'

'He felt betrayed, not only in 1998 but also in 1996 after his government fell. In view of his wide contacts across the political spectrum, Atal had felt that he would get support,' says senior journalist Kumar Ketkar. 'I had never seen Mr Vajpayee so dejected ever before. It was that [sic] he was sure he would continue to be the prime minister but had failed to [sic].'

NINE
Pursuing Peace

TWO MONTHS AFTER CONDUCTING nuclear tests, that catapulted India to the status of a nuclear-weapons state, Prime Minister Atal Bihari Vajpayee gave an interview to *India Today* on the nuclear testing.

> We conducted the series of nuclear tests keeping with our commitment made to people during the elections. It is part of the national agenda for governance. I have been advocating the cause of India going nuclear for the last four decades. My party has been making this demand consistently and forcefully. Now that we are in the government, people expect us to translate this long standing commitment into action. And we have showed them that we mean business.

The nuclear tests were conducted on 11–13 May 1998, less than two months after Atal came to power at the head of a coalition on 19 March 1998. The decision to go in for nuclear tests was among one of Atal's first moves. This was not without reason. With two weak preceding governments that had shaken the confidence of the people, Atal, who had headed a thirteen-day government in 1996, wanted to send the message that his regime was a strong one. In Atal's opinion, this purpose was served by the nuclear test because in the *India Today* interview he said, 'Millions of Indians have viewed this occasion as the beginning of the rise of a strong self-confident India.'

The tests were conducted in Pokhran, a small desert town in Rajasthan. The first nuclear tests, during the time of Indira Gandhi, had also been conducted there. The tests this time were more comprehensive. It now appears that to boost his sagging image, Narasimha Rao had also planned a nuclear test in 1995. However, American satellites, that keep a tab on developments across the world, had picked up signals about a possible test and the US administration had convinced the Rao government to abandon the idea. This meant that Atal's men had to conduct the test very carefully and ensure that there were no signs that a nuclear test was being planned. Extra precautions were taken by the nuclear scientists led by A.P.J. Abdul Kalam (later to become the president of India) and the army commanders who were involved in the operation. As a result, the world at large only knew about the tests after Atal hurriedly convened a press conference at his residence post the event. People in India reacted positively, and even the stock markets went up. The Congress party, however, alleged that political motivations had fuelled the test.

Not unexpectedly, the Americans and the western lobby were left red-faced. The US, in keeping with the nuclear non-proliferation treaty, imposed sanctions, cutting off all aid save that for humanitarian purposes and banned export of certain defence and other technology to India. Japan also imposed sanctions. Russia and France, however, refrained from saying anything negative about India. Not surprisingly, China reacted strongly and said that India had acted in an unreasonable manner and called upon the international community to take a unified stand and demand that India should immediately stop the development of nuclear weapons. Atal was unfazed.

He told *India Today* in the interview quoted earlier: 'Yes, the tests have entailed a price. But we should not worry about it. India has a reservoir of resources and inner strength. If we tap its reservoir, the benefit will be a hundred times more than any price that we may have to pay in the short run.'

In some senses India lost its advantage when, a fortnight later, on 28 May, Pakistan too conducted nuclear tests at Chagtai Hills. This prompted US President Bill Clinton to comment, 'Two wrongs don't make a right.'

Incidentally, after India conducted its tests, the Pakistani foreign minister had reacted by saying, 'Indian leadership has gone berserk and is acting in an unrestrained way.' However, the Pakistani prime minister Nawaz Sharif had said that his country would respond appropriately to the Indian tests.

Atal's mentor in the Bharatiya Jana Sangh, Deen Dayal Upadhyaya, in the mid-1960s (in conjunction with socialist leader Ram Manohar Lohia), had come up with the concept of a confederation of India and Pakistan. This concept, in a way, repudiated the one of Akhand Bharat that extreme right-wing Hindu organizations had been espousing, and paved the way for good bilateral relations between the two countries which could then present a joint front on many matters. Once India achieved its nuclear power status as did Pakistan, Atal felt that it was time that the two countries started working towards good relations. Atal's counterpart in Pakistan, Nawaz Sharif, also believed that the two countries should foster good relations. Sharif sent an invitation to Atal to visit Pakistan. Pakistan wanted to test the commitment of the new BJP government. Atal responded wholeheartedly and crossed the Attari–Wagah border in Punjab by bus on the afternoon of 19 February 1999. He was accompanied by twenty-two distinguished Indians who included journalists like Kuldeep Nayar, cultural personalities like Mallika Sarabhai and film personalities like Dev Anand and Javed Akhtar. The bus that Atal went by was to become a daily feature from Delhi to Lahore and back. The bus service was to foster better people-to-people contacts, including allowing families that lived on either side of the border to meet each other.

Immediately after crossing the border, where he was received by Nawaz Sharif, Atal said, 'This is a defining moment in South Asian history and we will have to rise to the challenge.' Atal's aide Sudheendra Kulkarni later recalled how Pakistani information minister Mushahid Hussain had said to him on the sidelines, 'Vajpayeeji has real guts to come to Pakistan like this and at this time.'

Hundreds of people had lined up at the border to witness this historic crossover. Talks between Atal and Sharif led to the Lahore declaration by which both countries pledged to a peaceful resolution of bilateral disputes, especially Kashmir, and fostering friendly commercial and cultural relationships. The declaration stated that the two sides would engage in bilateral consultations on security concepts, nuclear doctrines and avoidance of conflicts. The two countries agreed to give advance notification of ballistic missile flight tests and conclude bilateral agreements. They were also committed to undertaking national measures to reduce the risks of accidental or unauthorized incidents that could lead to a nuclear war.

More than anything else, Atal managed to charm the Pakistani public with his disarming ways, although fundamentalist organizations and parties launched public demonstrations against the his visit. Atal also visited the Minar-e-Pakistan during the trip, a monument set up in 1947 to commemorate the birth of the nation. Atal said that he had been dissuaded by many from visiting the minar because it would be tantamount to giving a stamp of approval to the creation of Pakistan.

'I insisted on coming because I saw no logic in what was being told to me and I made it loud and clear to them that Pakistan does not require my stamp for its entity. Pakistan has its own entity,' Atal said. He added, 'If somebody back home asks this question, this will be my answer there too.'

Incidentally, at a reception at Governor House, Atal recited his poem 'Ab jung naa hone denge hum'. Atal was felicitated at Lahore Fort where, hinting at the common heritage of the two nations, he pointed out how Shah Jahan was born in the fort and Akbar had spent close to a decade there. The audience was so impressed by Atal's speech that Nawaz Sharif quipped, '*Vajpayee sahab ab toh Pakistan mein bhi election jeet sakte hain*. [Mr Vajpayee can now win elections even in Pakistan.]'

Though there was no forward movement publicly on the thorny issue of Kashmir, privately it seems that Atal and Nawaz Sharif had agreed to resolve the issue once and for all. Atal was keen on a quick resolution and wanted to find a solution by the end of 1999; that meant within ten months. The two leaders also agreed that the preparations for the final agreement would be through Track II Diplomacy and not through foreign service officials who had their own fixed viewpoints (read biases).

Within days after returning to Delhi, Atal called Nawaz Sharif and asked him whether he was ready to move forward on Kashmir. When Sharif said yes, Atal nominated R.K. Mishra as his emissary and negotiator for the purpose. Mishra, the then chairman of the Observer group of newspapers and earlier the editor of the *Patriot*, was an influential man in New Delhi's policy circles. Nawaz Sharif also nominated a representative, Anwar Zahid, who unfortunately died within ten days of his nomination, in which time one meeting was held. Thereafter, Sharif put Pakistan's retired foreign secretary and former high commissioner to India, Niaz Naik, on the job.

The two representatives had many meetings in close succession, alternately in Delhi and Islamabad, and are believed to have had good talks. The talks were directed from behind the stage by Atal on the Indian side and Nawaz Sharif on the Pakistani side. The basic elements for the deliberations were guided by the agreement that both sides should move forward publicly beyond their stated positions on Kashmir. Further, a solution to the Kashmir problem must take into account the interests of India, Pakistan and *above all* the Kashmiri people (the words 'above all' were inserted at the instance of Atal). It was also agreed that the solution to the Kashmir problem must be fair and feasible. Atal was emphatic and wanted that 'the agreed solution to Kashmir must be final and not partial'. He also made it clear that a referendum on Kashmir was ruled out as was UN trusteeship of Kashmir. He gave a brief to his representative that the talks should result in a 'new and innovative solution' to the problem. Once, in between the talks (when the meeting was being held in Delhi), Atal wanted to meet the Pakistani representative Niaz Naik. Atal asked Naik, when the latter called on him, that he should go back home and tell Nawaz Sharif that whenever infiltration had started from the Pakistani side in the summer months, shelling across the line of control (LOC) soon followed. Atal told Naik to tell Sharif to ensure that in the ensuing summers this pattern was not repeated, at least as far as possible.

Niaz Naik went back home, called on Sharif and briefed him about the talks, which had so far been carried out in total secrecy, such that virtually nobody was aware of the negotiations. On hearing out Naik, Sharif told him to brief the Inter-Services Intelligence (ISI) and the army. As a result, Naik immediately hastened to the ISI headquarters and briefed the top boss. A day later he called on the army chief of staff Pervez Musharraf and also told him about the talks. This was in the first week of April 1999. Incidentally, Musharraf and the chiefs of staff of the air force and navy had kept away from Wagah when Nawaz Sharif had received the visiting Atal. This was to signal that the armed forces were not so enthusiastic about the peace talks with India, although they had conjured up some excuses for their absence.

Musharraf had been appointed chief of the Pakistani armed forces in October 1998 and it seems that he, in collaboration with a few top army bosses, had hatched a plan to foment trouble in Kashmir. This was to take 'revenge' on the Indian 'occupation' of the Siachen glacier from where the Pakistanis had not been able to dislodge the Indians since 1984. During winters, when temperatures reached sub-zero levels, soldiers from both the sides retreated from their hilltop positions, only to return next summer. This had been the practice for many years. However, in the spring of 1999, when Indian soldiers were yet to reoccupy the heights in the Kargil region, Pakistani soldiers occupied their heights and also the Indian heights. The Kargil region is 200 km from Srinagar. The hilltops of Kargil are strategically located because they overlook the highway that runs from Srinagar to Leh and thus connects Ladakh to the Kashmir valley. Therefore, if Pakistani troops could shell the highway from the hilltops, they could cut off communication lines to Leh, the capital of Ladakh. Incidentally, Kargil was just 170 km from Skardu in Pakistan-occupied Kashmir (POK), therefore the soldiers could be serviced by the Pakistanis from not too distant a place. In the event, soldiers of the Northern Light Infantry (NLI) and the special service group of the Pakistani army occupied the heights. Indian army patrol parties became fully cognizant of the infiltration after being tipped off by local shepherds in the second week of May.

To Atal it was clear that on one side the Pakistanis were talking peace and on the other hand they were pursuing aggression. Nawaz Sharif later said that he was not aware of these occurrences and came to know of them only when Atal called him telephonically and informed him. Pakistan continued to maintain that the men who had occupied the Indian heights were not Pakistani army men but Kashmiri freedom fighters. About two years later, Musharraf said that Nawaz knew everything and had been briefed fifteen days before Atal's trip to Pakistan. How far this is true remains a matter of speculation.

The Indian army, with cover support from the air force, launched Operation Vijay in May 1999 and was able to clear the Pakistani infiltrators and reclaim the heights on 26 July 1999. At one stage, after being pressured by the Clinton administration, Nawaz Sharif ordered the Pakistan army to vacate the heights. Though the men of the NLI heeded his orders and retreated, the irregulars did not listen to him. The US government was wary of the Pakistani moves because of the apprehension that the country in desperation could use the nuclear option. Sharif was ordered to come to Washington, where he was given a dressing down.

With the outbreak of the Kargil operations, it became doubly clear that the Pakistani army was not keen on the peace process and, in fact, had stepped up infiltration the moment it had learnt about the negotiations. Atal also realized that no peace process could be taken forward without taking the Pakistani army on board. Whatever be his realization, more bad news was awaiting him on the Pakistan front.

On 24 December 1999, on Christmas Eve and also a day before Atal's birthday, an Indian Airlines flight, IC 814 from Kathmandu to New Delhi, was hijacked by five armed militants soon after the plane entered Indian airspace. The militants, all of whom were later identified as Pakistanis, forced the plane to go to Lahore. But the Pakistani authorities, who wanted to demonstrate that they had nothing to do with the hijacking, would not allow the flight to land there. So the pilot brought it to Amritsar's Raja Sansi airport with very little fuel. The plane had 178 passengers and eleven crew members on board.

Atal, meanwhile, was airborne in an Indian Air Force (IAF)

Boeing and had no clue about the happenings. He was returning from somewhere in southern India and the plane had no satellite phone. He was given the information on landing in Delhi at 7 p.m., an hour and forty minutes after the incident. Due to the late receipt of the information, Atal could not react as well as he could have had the information reached him on time. The ideal thing would have been to airship commandos of the National Security Guard (NSG) to Amritsar from their headquarters at Manesar near Delhi. But this did not happen. The plane was on the tarmac for forty-five minutes and the ideal thing to do was to somehow keep it on Indian soil. The hijackers, fearing a commando operation, stabbed a young passenger, Rupin Katyal, who was returning with his wife from a honeymoon, and forced the pilot to get airborne with a virtually empty fuel tank. Atal and his men could do nothing, although foreign minister Jaswant Singh kept barking orders on the phone to Amritsar airport authorities to somehow block the runaway with a heavy vehicle. The plane went to Lahore, where the lights had been put off, including those on the runway, to prevent it from landing. However, the plane landed successfully, thanks to the dexterity of the pilot.

The next morning, after being refuelled it flew to Dubai. On Atal's instructions, External Affairs Minister Jaswant Singh had called his Pakistani counterpart for help, but to no avail. The Pakistanis were strangely not receptive to the problem. After some negotiations and the release of thirteen women, eleven children and the offloading of the body of Rupin Katyal (who had bled to death by then), the plane took off from Dubai. It landed in Kandahar in Taliban territory. The hijackers then made a demand for the release of thirty-six terrorists lodged in various Indian jails.

A few days later, after countless rounds of negotiations, three dreaded terrorists, accompanied by Jaswant Singh, were ferried to Kandahar in a plane and released in exchange for the hostages.

One of the terrorists released was Masood Azhar, who many years later organized the 26/11 attacks on Mumbai, and another was Omar Sheikh, who killed American journalist Daniel Pearl. The whole hijacking incident brought in its wake a controversy about the way the Atal government had dealt with the crisis. Would the plane have been allowed to take off from Amritsar if some VIPs had been on board? Analysts asked whether the Atal government had reacted competently and professionally to the crisis. It also brought into sharp focus the intentions of the Pakistani government.

Even after so many setbacks, Atal had not given up his dream of peace between India and Pakistan. Foreign affairs was his passion and he wanted to make a lasting impression on India–Pakistan relations. The circumstances, however, were not favourable. A disappointed Atal, in his musings from Kumarakom (where he had gone for a New Year sojourn, at the end of 2000 and beginning of 2001) wrote, 'India is willing and ready to seek a lasting solution to the Kashmir problem. We are prepared to recommence talks with Pakistan at any level including the highest level, provided Islamabad gives sufficient proof of its preparedness to create a conducive atmosphere. On Kashmir, we shall not traverse on [sic] the beaten path of the past.'

Seeing his deep desire to restore peace with Pakistan, Advani one day told Atal that he should take the initiative once again. External Affairs Minister Jaswant Singh, who was also present, seconded the proposal and thereby the idea of a new peace process was initiated.

An invitation was sent to Parvez Musharraf, who was now the president of his country, having deposed Nawaz Sharif in a coup. Although Musharraf was the architect of Kargil, Atal averred that as the head of the country with no political constituency to address, the general had the flexibility of taking a decision that a politician could not dare to. Musharraf was enthusiastic in accepting the invitation. He was a showman and wanted to use the opportunity to do his public relations in India. Moreover, he wanted to visit his ancestral home in Delhi's Daryaganj, where he had been born before his family had migrated to Pakistan during partition.

The meetings were scheduled in Agra between 14 and 16 July 2001. The choice of venue was made by Atal. He thought it would be appropriately for the capital of the Mughals to host the talks. The original choice was Goa, but Atal had it changed. It soon become clear that Musharraf was hellbent on charting his own course. To start with, he had a controversial meeting with Kashmiri separatist leaders. Hours before his visit to Delhi, there was violence on the Indo-Pak border with the troops of both countries exchanging fire. This was the first time in 2001 that this was happening. The second day of the visit was marked by violence and eighteen people died in Kashmir in fights between mercenaries from across the border and Indian troops.

Meanwhile, in Agra, the general was playing more games. Although Indian ministers like L.K. Advani, Jaswant Singh, Sushma Swaraj and Yashwant Sinha were in Agra to assist Atal, they were tight-lipped while the general was at his garrulous best. He called for an off-the-record breakfast meeting with senior Indian journalists that was broadcast live. Here the general spoke his mind and his utterances did not amuse Atal and his ministers.

In substantive terms, differences cropped up between the Indian and Pakistani sides because of the former's insistence on focusing on the issue of cross-border terrorism that had become big with the turn of the century. For Pakistan, Kashmir was the central issue and the rest was peripheral. Cross-border terrorism was not an issue for the general because according to him it was Kashmiri freedom fighters fighting Indian security forces.

In the end, the two sides differed so much that even a joint statement could not be finalized. Musharraf, who was to visit the dargah of Khwaja Moinuddin Chisti in Ajmer, abandoned the trip and flew off to Pakistan in a huff. In 2010, he blamed a joint secretary in the Indian external affairs ministry, Vivek Katju, of mischief. Katju was an Atal confidant and had been invited to the one-on-one meeting between the Indian prime minister and Pakistani president. Katju was furiously taking down notes and Musharraf suspected his motives in doing so. Musharraf said that while leaving Agra, 'I told Vajpayee Saheb, today you and I both have been humiliated because there is someone above us who can veto whatever we decide.' This was also a reference to Advani who had apparently raised questions on a draft joint statement that been finalized by Indian foreign minister Jaswant Singh and the foreign minister of Pakistan. This was at an impromptu cabinet meeting that Atal convened in his hotel suite in Agra. Though Jaswant had agreed to the draft statement, it had no reference to cross-border terrorism. The insistence of Pakistan on not mentioning this matter meant that a joint statement could not be made.

The Pakistani official spokesman, while addressing the press, said that a draft joint statement had been readied but could not be announced because a 'hidden hand' had sabotaged it. Sections of the Pakistani press later came up with other explanations of why the talks could not be successful. They claimed that the talks between the two countries followed a gentle prodding by US president Bill Clinton in 2000. The talks started at the non-governmental level with Musharraf's brother, Dr Naved, on the Pakistani side and retired Admiral K.K. Nayar on the Indian side. Later, from the Indian side, Pramod Mahajan and Atal's son-in-law, Ranjan Bhattacharya, also came into the picture. Meetings took place in Chicago, Europe and Hong Kong. In the end, an informal agreement was thrashed out whereby Pakistan agreed to stop cross-border terrorism and India promised 'real autonomy' to Kashmir at a later date that would be specified. Pakistan would also give right of way for an Indo-Iran oil pipeline. It was to sign such an agreement that Musharraf was coming to India. The applecart was upset when Advani, who did not know about the nitty-gritties of the informal agreement, jumped into the fray and expressed objections to the deal. He did this at the instance of the RSS chief K.S. Sudarshan, Pakistani press reports claimed. They also asserted that Musharraf was shocked when what he thought was a 'done deal' did not materialize. That was why he left Agra in a huff.

A few months later, on 13 December 2001, there was a terrorist attack on Indian Parliament. Gunmen armed with AK-47s, rocket launchers, pistols and grenades entered the Parliament complex in a car with home ministry labels and began indiscriminate firing. Though the gunmen could not enter Parliament House, six Delhi police personnel, two watch and ward officials of Parliament and a gardener were killed before the gunmen were shot down. L.K. Advani gave a statement in Parliament the next day: 'We have received clues which shows [sic] a neighbouring country and some terrorist organizations active there are behind the attack.' A demarche was also issued to the Pakistani high commissioner in Delhi, advising his government to curb activities of terrorist organizations in Pakistan, apprehend their leaders and freeze their financial assets. Pakistan responded by issuing a high alert. India also amassed its forces on the border in what was the biggest mobilization since the 1971 war and the Pakistanis followed suit. The two armies, in full battle preparedness, stood eyeball to eyeball for a few months.

Atal was a peacenik. Thus, he did not give up his dream to usher in permanent peace with Pakistan. In fact, he was so resolute that those not so close to him started to snigger that the prime minister was harping on peace only with the objective of getting a Nobel Prize for peace. Insiders say that Atal heard these murmurs and apparently laughed them off, saying that he was seeking peace for India and not a Nobel Prize for himself. Accordingly Atal proposed, once again in April 2003, that India was ready to normalize relations with Pakistan on the basis of 'trust and sincerity'. General

Musharraf responded that he was ready for unconditional talks, but India said that the first thing was that Pakistan should not allow terrorist attacks from its soil. Realizing that the 2001 talks had gone for a toss, because official-level preparatory talks did not precede the talks between Atal and Musharraf, this time the Indian side wanted to proceed gingerly and step by step.

In November 2003, India offered a set of confidence-building measures (CBM) including restoration of stalled air, rail and sea links, as well as sporting links like cricketing ties. More buses between Delhi and Lahore were proposed and a new bus between Srinagar and Muzaffarabad in POK was put on the table. In January 2004, when Atal went to Pakistan for the SAARC (South Asian Association for Regional Cooperation) meeting, a joint statement was issued expressing the intent to hold a composite dialogue between the two countries. Atal said that he was confident that resumption of the composite dialogue would lead to a peaceful settlement of bilateral issues including that of Jammu & Kashmir to the satisfaction of both sides. General Musharraf also assured that he would not allow any territory under Pakistan's control to be used for terrorism in any manner.

The composite dialogue could, however, not get going in Atal's tenure because elections were called early and the results pushed his government out of power. Although Atal could not achieve lasting peace with Pakistan, his intentions can never be doubted. In fact, Alex Perry wrote in *TIME* magazine, on 26 April 2004, that Atal's plan to 'visit Pakistan to talk with Musharraf in Islamabad and the agreement to end half a century of war and hostility' had only one parallel in modern history and that was Egyptian President Anwar Sadat's 1977 mission to Jerusalem.

Needless to add, Atal's tenure also saw a high in relations with the US, which during the Cold War period, had been in cold storage. With the end of the Cold War, a new approach was visible from the US. President Bill Clinton visited India in March 2000 for a five-day visit. This was the first visit by a US president in twenty-two years. Clinton recognized India's rise as a software power and with the rise of Taliban, the US was willing to downgrade the importance of Pakistan in South Asia and push up India. Atal, cognizant of the importance of the USA, visited the country five times during his tenure, including twice in 2001. His first visit was in September 2000 and he put Jaswant Singh in charge of getting into the nitty-gritties of the relationship. Jaswant Singh held talks with US deputy secretary of state, Strobe Talbot. Twelve rounds of negotiations were held in different parts of the world between June 1998 and February 2001. These helped normalize relations between the two countries. A very comprehensive and futuristic bilateral agreement was signed, setting the tone for relations between the two biggest democracies in the world. Outlined in detail were schemes and mechanisms for cooperation between the two countries in many areas including economic and security. As a result, an Indo-US financial and economic forum was established as was a US–India commercial dialogue, a US–India working group in trade and a US–India science and technology forum. With the benefit of hindsight, analysts now say that it was Atal who paved the path for the 'two estranged democracies to become natural allies'.

Atal was conscious that although he was trying to build a new relationship with the US, existing relations could not be disturbed. Russia had a long and enduring association with India and had supported the country through thick and thin. Russian President Vladimir Putin visited India in October 2000 to strengthen relations and this was followed by Atal's visit to Russia in November 2001. A Moscow declaration was signed, and this enabled continuation of closer relations on trade and security.

TEN

Dealing with the Alma Mater

ON THE EVE OF the formation of his ministry in March 1998, Atal had a surprise midnight visitor. It was K.S. Sudarshan, the number two person in the RSS. Though the exact details of the conversation that night between Atal and Sudarshan are not known, the latter told the prime minister to keep Jaswant Singh out of the cabinet that was being formed. Jaswant had been the finance minister in Atal's thirteen-day ministry in 1996, and was widely expected to be appointed as the custodian of the important ministry headquartered in central secretariat's North Block once again. Sudarshan's logic was that Jaswant had lost the just-concluded elections, and it was not in the right democratic spirit to appoint him a minister. Atal was a little flummoxed and annoyed too, if insiders are to be believed. However, he fell in line with the diktat from the RSS. The next day, when the cabinet was announced, the name of Jaswant Singh was missing from the list, sparking widespread speculation. Insiders say that the RSS had reservations about Jaswant Singh because he was an outsider. In a BJP that was full of RSS men seconded to the political party, the former army major who had been to the elite Mayo College in Ajmer was an exception. Jaswant Singh had never been in the RSS. In the corridors of the BJP's Ashoka Road office, there was a lot of gossip about Jaswant's lifestyle which was far from being spartan and there were allegations floating about how he was close to a particular business house. Nothing was proven, but obviously Nagpur had harped on his failure to win the Lok Sabha polls to ensure that he did not make the ministerial grade.

Atal was not a man to take things lying down, and he appointed Jaswant Singh as the deputy chairman of the Planning Commission within days and got him elected to the Rajya Sabha in July 1998. A few months later, in December, Jaswant was inducted into the cabinet, but as defence minister. Some years later, in 2002, he was made finance minister.

Although Sudarshan is believed to have used the name of RSS sarsanghchalak Rajendra Singh to put forward the 'request' to deny Jaswant a cabinet berth, Atal instinctively knew that it was Sudarshan's own ploy. He knew that Sudarshan had convinced the RSS top boss to issue a diktat. From that day, Atal made strenuous efforts to keep Sudarshan at bay. Atal had good relations with Rajendra Singh, going beyond the fact that both belonged to the cow-belt. Rajendra Singh, who was only three years older than Atal, had been acquainted with the latter since the mid-1940s. Rajendra Singh, a former professor of physics at Allahabad University and the first non-Brahmin to head the RSS, held Atal—and more so, 'Brand Atal'—in high regard. Atal knew that if Rajendra Singh continued as RSS sarsanghchalak, he would manage the BJP government's relationship with Nagpur quite well. However, Rajendra Singh, better known as Rajju bhaiyya, had expressed his desire to step down because of bad health and pass on the mantle to Sudarshan. There was a more senior contender, H.V. Seshadri, but he was suffering from a heart ailment. Atal was apprehensive of Sudarshan, a Kannadiga who had grown up in Chattisgarh's (formerly a part of Madhya Pradesh) Raipur region. Sudarshan was too conservative and propagated the cause of swadeshi at a time when the economy was being freed. In fact, Atal held that Sudarshan's reservations about Jaswant as finance minister also stemmed from the fact that the latter was seen as a liberalizer. According to Hindutva expert Jyotirmaya Sharma, Atal spent the next two years convincing Rajendra Singh that he continue and not step down. In this endeavour, he pressed even his colleague L.K. Advani into service, Sharma claims. But in March 2000, Rajendra Singh ultimately stepped down, his health deteriorating. Sudarshan took over and for the next two years, till the Gujarat riots happened, Atal kept the new sarsanghchalak at bay. To all his requests Atal told Sudarshan that he would have been happy to oblige, but for the fact that the government that he headed was not a BJP but an NDA dispensation and there was no way that the alliance partners would agree.

'Advani, at the behest of Atal, would invite Sudarshan and his colleague M.G. Vaidya to dinner at home and convince them how what they were seeking was impossible to do,' says Sharma.

The fact that Atal was at least a decade senior to Sudarshan in the RSS made it possible for him to keep the sarsanghchalak from interfering in government decisions. In Atal's eyes, the RSS supremo was no revered individual whose word was Atal's command. Journalist H.K. Dua, who for some time was Prime Minister Atal Bihari Vajpayee's public relations advisor, recollects how Atal told him not to bother about the RSS.

'I had taken a strong line against the demolition of the Babri Masjid as the editor of the *Hindustan Times* and I expressed my concern to Atalji on how the RSS would take to my appointment. He said, "You don't bother about the RSS, I know how to manage them."'

The Jana Sangh, the predecessor of the Bharatiya Janata Party, was founded by Shyama Prasad Mukherjee in 1951 as an independent party, although he wanted the cooperation of the RSS. To begin with, the RSS kept the Jana Sangh at arm's length, merely providing it with a few volunteers. This was not surprising considering that the sarsanghchalak, M.S. Golwalkar, was not deeply interested in politics, at least not of the power-seeking kind. The objective of the RSS was to spread cultural nationalism. However, after the premature death of Shyama Prasad, the RSS took control of the Jana Sangh. This was after the next president of the Jana Sangh, Mouli Chandra Sharma, started taking steps that the RSS felt were making the party look like the Congress. Control over the Jana Sangh was taken through the secretary of the party, Deen Dayal Upadhyaya.

On 25 June 1956, three years after Shyama Prasad's death, Golwalkar wrote in the *Organiser*, elucidating the RSS point of view, 'I had to warn him [Shyama Prasad] that the RSS could not be drawn into politics; that it could not play second fiddle to any political or other party, since no organization devoted to the wholesale regeneration of the real, that is cultural life of a nation could ever function if it was used as a handmaid [sic] of political parties.'

As recounted in an earlier chapter, Atal had Deen Dayal Upadhyaya's blessings and, through his good offices, Golwalkar's; and thus, he rose fast in the party.

'Atal was soon to be a poster boy of the RSS—a young man who was a great orator. Golwalkar came to believe that this was the kind of person that the Jana Sangh needed to expand fast. Golwalkar was aware of Atal's weaknesses when he was appointed as president of the Jana Sangh, but chose to ignore them because in his opinion he was the ideal man to lead the party,' says an old-time party insider who wishes to remain anonymous.

All this gave Atal leverage to pursue his independent line while at the same time showing respect to the RSS bosses.

After Golwalkar passed away in 1973, the next sarsanghchalak was Balasaheb Deoras, a decade older than Atal and a contemporary of Deen Dayal Upadhyaya's (who by then had passed away). Deoras's stewardship in the beginning posed no problem for Atal. Deoras was appreciative of Jayaprakash Narayan who, with his call for sampurna kranti, wanted to form a democratic front to oppose Indira Gandhi. The front, that was a coalition of all the opposition forces and had come into being because of the extraordinary circumstances of the Emergency, also had the blessings of Deoras. It is only after the Janata government fell and the Jana Sangh metamorphosed into the Bharatiya Janata Party that Atal began to face problems with the RSS top rung. In fact, just fifteen days after the Janata Party's Morarji Desai government fell, Atal wrote a piece on 2 August 1979 in the *Indian Express* where he stoutly defended the RSS but openly offered advice to the organization worthies about how to conduct themselves. He wrote that the RSS had nothing to do with communal violence in the country and the apprehensions about it aiming to capture political power were without foundation. Atal also said that the RSS issue that rocked the Morarji government was assiduously fuelled by some followers of Charan Singh as retaliation for the firm refusal of the erstwhile Jana Sangh members to destabilize the centre. At the same time, Atal also advised that journals connected with the RSS should not take sides in the power games going on in the political arena. He also said that the RSS should not be involved in youth bodies that interacted with political parties or with trade unions. He significantly advised the RSS to formally enunciate its accepted stand that by Hindu Rashtra it meant Bharatiya Rashtra.

The RSS was hardly amused at this open advice rendered by Atal. But what led to the beginning of the formal sidelining of the BJP president was his insistence on modelling the newly formed party on the principles of Gandhian socialism. Deoras now increasingly began to depend on the till then inert VHP to propagate the cultural objectives of the RSS. He also lent support to Indira Gandhi's Congress, that was perceived to be furthering the Hindu cause more fervently than the BJP.

A remorseful Atal, after losing the Lok Sabha elections held after the assassination of Indira Gandhi, said in Gwalior (from where he had contested) that he wanted to clear any misgivings: 'As a student of class X, I had written "*Hindu Tan Man, Hindu Jeevan, Rag Rag Hindu Mera Parichay*." People say that Atal, who had written the poem, is not the same who does politics. There is no truth in it. I am Hindu. How can I forget that? However, my Hindutva is not constricted, it is not narrow.'

The import of these words was recognized by Rajendra Singh when he became the RSS chief a decade later in 1994, after Deoras retired due to ill health. It was during the tenure of Rajendra Singh that Advani conceded that Atal and not he would be a better prime ministerial candidate. It is on the prompting of Rajendra Singh that Atal's persona was projected during the 1996 elections although, by its nature, the RSS is against a personality cult. The projection of Atal was a wise thing to do because the BJP connect with the RSS was still being used by opposition parties to berate the saffron party. Every time, however, Atal rose to the defence of the RSS. For instance, on 27 May 1996, when the short-lived Atal government was sought to be replaced by Deve Gowda, Atal said on the floor of the Lok Sabha that the RSS was an organization that was wedded to the cause of the nation. He gave two examples, one of the Republic Day parade of 1963 (after the Chinese debacle) when the RSS was one of the organizations invited to send in representatives to participate in the march past to demonstrate national unity. The other one related to 1965 when, at the time of the Indo-Pak war, the government had deployed RSS men to regulate traffic on the roads of Delhi. Atal went on to quote Deve Gowda who, while speaking at a function in Bangalore in the midst of the Emergency, had said, 'RSS is a spotless organization.' Atal added that the RSS was an independent organization and while 'you can differ with the RSS, the allegations against them are not required'.

Much of the problem that the Atal government had with Sudarshan was that he planted himself in Delhi permanently. Thus, he was freely available to the national media. Further, the RSS worthy did not shy away from commenting on various matters concerning state policies. Earlier, the RSS bosses used to operate out of Nagpur, far from Delhi; and even Rajendra Singh spent a lot of time in Allahabad, which was not too close to the national capital. He, of course, lived in Delhi too. Journalist Ashok Malik writing in *India Today* (7 May 2000) quoted a senior minister to describe Sudarshan as: 'Never a diplomat, rarely short of an answer and always accessible.' In the same article, he referred to many micro matters that Sudarshan had sought to intervene in, including the policy of direct-to-home (DTH) telecast, recommendation for Rajya Sabha candidates and even seeking expunging of comments in the annual confidential report of an officer from the north-east (whose boss was apparently biased and thus had written unfair comments). He also directly approached Atal after a VHP sympathizer was asked for a bribe by a lowly clerk of the Delhi Development Authority.

However, in the beginning of January 2000, when Rajendra Singh was still the RSS sarsanghchalak, Atal was put in a spot by a decision by Keshubhai Patel, BJP chief minister of Gujarat, to rescind a ban on state government employees being members of the RSS. The decision was taken just on the eve of an RSS meeting in the state capital Gandhinagar, attended even by the RSS sarsanghchalak. Keshubhai had, however, done his homework well because he had consulted the union home ministry on the matter a few months earlier and the ministry, headed by L.K. Advani, had noted that the Unlawful Activities Prevention Tribunal had, in 1993, found nothing unlawful in the activities of the RSS. However, Keshubhai's move had the entire opposition and even the partners of the BJP in the NDA government in Delhi up in arms.

The beginning of the budget session in February 2000 was marked by pandemonium, and Atal was pressed by the Lok Sabha Speaker G.M.C. Balayogi to intervene. In March, finding himself under pressure, Atal got Advani to intervene with the BJP President Kushabhau Thakre to use his good offices to get Keshubhai to withdraw the enabling order. Thakre, it was believed, would be effective because he was a hardcore RSS man. However, Keshubhai was adamant and wanted Thakre to talk to the RSS bosses in Nagpur first. This was even after Rajendra Singh had obliquely hinted that the RSS would not be unduly perturbed by the withdrawal of the order enabling government employees to participate in the organization's activities because it was not dependent for its growth on 'official patronage'. In the end, however, the Gujarat government withdrew the orders in March 2000 after much cajoling, but this was one matter in which Atal had been cornered before he could get his way. Incidentally, the Gujarat government's original move was orchestrated not by Keshubhai but his home minister, Haren Pandya, who was known to be a close protégé of Advani's. Interestingly, Advani, elected to the Lok Sabha from Gujarat, was in fact one of the dignitaries who attended the RSS meeting in Gandhinagar, a day after the ban was lifted in January 2000. This incident shows the sort of pressure Atal was under from extreme elements in the RSS as well as from within the BJP, who were perfectly in tune with Nagpur. However, Atal managed it all in the end.

As far as Sudarshan was concerned, Atal was able to get him off his back and in fact dispatch him back to Nagpur, which is where the headquarters of the RSS was located in April 2000. A year later, Atal obliquely targeted the RSS top bosses while addressing the condolence meeting held for Rajendra Singh on 26 July 2003 at New Delhi's Talkatora Stadium. He said, 'What was special about

Rajju bhaiyya was that we could discuss divergent views with him on different subjects. A time comes after taking different views expressed for discussions, a final view is taken. But that never led to any bitterness.' This quote appeared in a report carried in the *Telegraph,* headlined, 'Atal gives Sangh a lesson in diversity'.

More commonly known is the way Atal dealt with K.N. Govindacharya, the general secretary of the BJP. An RSS pracharak, Govindacharya had been inducted into the BJP to infuse dynamism in the party that was then being energized by L.K. Advani. Govindacharya was the man who conceived of Advani's rath yatra and also pushed for a policy of involving OBCs in the party. Atal, however, disliked him. This was not surprising, considering that it was precisely during the time that the RSS inductee was helping Advani that Atal was sidelined. Atal got his chance when an article written in a Hindi publication by Bhanu Pratap Shukla, former editor of *Panchajanya,* claimed that Govindacharya had, at a meeting with three British diplomats, described Vajpayee as the party's mukhota (mask) while the real power lay with Advani. Atal complained and Govindacharya retracted, saying that he had never used such words. He said that he had great respect for Atal, who was the party's mukut (crown) and pagri (turban). Atal was in no mood to pardon Govindacharya, and had the latter banished. Insiders say that Atal did not want to overlook this incident, notwithstanding Govindacharya's denial, because he felt that continuing with the latter would give a wrong impression about the power equation within the party and also between the party and the RSS. Importantly, Govindacharya was also a strong supporter of the Swadeshi Jagran Manch that opposed the policies of liberalization.

That Atal was allergic to the allegation that he worked under the RSS's pressure is very clear from how he reacted to Leader of Opposition Sonia Gandhi's contentions on the floor of Parliament, when he went virtually ballistic. On 26 March 2002, when a joint session of Parliament was convened to pass the Prevention of Terrorism Act (POTA), Sonia Gandhi said, '*PMji aapka waqt aa gaya hai. Aap ko kursi ki garima bachaani hogi athava Sangh Parivar ke dabaav mein kaam karna hoga. Aapki ganana ka waqt aa gaya hai* [Mr PM, your time has come. You have to decide whether you want to uphold the dignity of your office or work as per the dictates of the Sangh Parivar. It is time for your reckoning].'

A livid Atal answered, '*Main aisi charcha mein nahin padna chahta* [I do not want to be drawn into such discussions].' He added:

> It is alleged that I work under pressure. I do not work under anybody's pressure. Your party under pressure stopped nuclear tests. The dates were ready and the preparations had been made. But under foreign pressure the tests were stopped. But we went ahead with the nuclear tests in spite of the pressures. When we were fighting in Kargil, Clinton pressured us to talk to Pakistan. But we said that so long as Pakistan holds one cent of our land we will not talk. What does Soniaji want to say? When she was in Italy I had started doing parliamentary work. I know about my countrymen more than you. Who are you to tell about the Sangh Parivar pressure? This is an internal Parivar matter. *Aap dakhal mat dijiye.*

Not all BJP insiders endorse the way Atal dealt with the RSS once in power. A party organization man, who feels bitter that he was kept out of important positions in the government, says that once the BJP came to power, power brokers made a beeline for party leaders in the government. Even people who had lately entered the party, got accommodated in important positions through their manoeuvring. He says that leaders who were always at the party headquarters became scarce. In these circumstances, he asks, was it wrong for Sudarshan to keep a check on government policies and priorities by offering continual advice?

On the other side, the Atal viewpoint, expounded by one of his former close aides, is that running a government, that too a coalition government with disparate parties, is not an easy task. 'Continual advice is like pinpricking. Independence and autonomy is necessary for running the government. That's what boss [Atal] did. He was every inch an RSS man, but was pragmatic enough to know where to stop the busy bodies of the RSS.'

Those who have known Atal for years say that for him the RSS was his alma mater where he had learnt the lessons of life and which had made a man of him. He once wrote, '[the] Sangh is my soul'. But as a practical man, he was not ready to be dictated to by the Sangh on every move that he made and every step that he took. What made him successfully resist the pressure from the RSS was the fact that he was head and shoulders above all those who could challenge him in the BJP and the Jana Sangh before that. Moreover, there was nobody in the RSS who could be seconded to the party to challenge him.

A case in point is Nanaji Deshmukh, an RSS man who built the Jana Sangh through his assiduous efforts in UP. Largely responsible for the elevation of Atal as the president of the Jana Sangh, for a few years thereafter Nanaji closely assisted him in gaining ground in the party. However, the two drifted apart and in the end Nanaji quit the party altogether and settled to a life of rural development in Chitrakoot, on the border of UP and Madhya Pradesh. Nanaji, an extremely capable organization man, realized that there was no way that he could handle Atal, even though the latter had won the first Lok Sabha polls in Balrampur only because of the work done on the ground by him.

After the Gujarat riots of 2002, however, Atal seems to have lost out to the RSS. The organization gained ascendancy with the help of hardliners in the party as also the Sangh Parivar. The first indication of this came on 4 April 2002, when Atal visited Gujarat after the bloody riots in which one thousand people lost their lives. The riots had followed the burning of the compartment of a train that was bringing back kar sevaks from Ayodhya. The incident had happened on 27 February 2002. At a press conference Atal, with the Gujarat chief minister Narendra Modi by his side, said that the government's job was to practise rajadharma and kings and rulers cannot discriminate between people on the basis of birth, caste and religion. Unexpectedly, in what was seen as a snub, Modi said, *'Wohi toh nibha rahein hain* [That's what we are doing].' The audience was shocked and Atal kept quiet.

Atal, disquieted with the way the Gujarat riots had been handled, decided to get rid of Modi at the national executive of the party scheduled a week later at Goa. As per the plan, in a face saver for Modi, he would submit his resignation at Goa and would be allowed to quit. On the flight to Goa, tremendous pressure was exerted on Atal by Advani to not accept Modi's resignation. Somehow word about the proposal for Modi to resign had leaked out. Young and mid-level leaders of the party started raising slogans, *'Istifa mat do, istifa mat do* [Don't quit, don't quit],' the moment Modi stood up to resign. In fact, a resolution was passed that Modi and his government had done their best while facing the challenge during the riots. Thus Atal was stymied. Modi, as is widely known, was a core RSS man who had become the chief minister of a state without being a legislator or an MP.

Two months later, in July 2002, Advani was elevated as deputy prime minister. Though Advani's well-wishers had been lobbying in party circles, from the very beginning in 1999, for him to become deputy prime minister, Atal had resisted. In fact, Atal had propped up a wall of moderate leaders around him. These included Jaswant Singh and Brajesh Mishra, who besides being Atal's principal secretary was also the national security advisor. George Fernandes, a minister but not from the BJP, had been given an important position and Atal also took the support of Nitish Kumar and the Andhra Pradesh chief minister, Chandrababu Naidu, to keep the RSS lobby at bay. He had also ensured low-key presidents for the BJP, many of whom like Bangaru Laxman, who had served the Atal government as a minister of state, had no independent standing. Others like Jana Krishnamurthi and Venkaiah Naidu came from states (Tamil Nadu and Andhra Pradesh respectively) where the BJP had little support among the electorate. Atal took the line that these leaders were being installed so that they could make a difference in the vote base in their states. However, this was a thinly veiled tactic to place weak leaders, who could not even get elected from their own states much less challenge Atal, at the top.

In October 2002, a few months after Atal had made a failed bid to make Modi resign, the RSS demanded a high-level meeting with government representatives and the BJP. This was to review the working of the government and decide on a mid-term course correction. As per newspaper reports of that time, the three major areas where correction was sought were economic policies, which the RSS considered too liberal and anti-Swadeshi; Pakistan, where it said that the government had not been able to counter the moves of that country; and the Ram temple issue. Atal, Advani and Venkaiah Naidu, the BJP president, met a team consisting of the RSS boss K.S. Sudarshan, joint general secretary H.V. Seshadri and Madan Das Devi. Although the talks were inconclusive, more importantly, the RSS had got Atal to the discussion table officially, and this is what mattered.

On the Ram temple issue, the RSS launched a new offensive for building the temple directly as well as through its affiliate, the VHP, from the beginning of 2003. VHP general secretary Giriraj Kishore openly called Atal a 'pseudo Hindu' who was not assisting in the Ram temple issue, while the VHP supremo Ashok Singhal declared that Atal was inebriated with power and that he should resign if he could not bring in legislation for the construction of the Ram temple. At the beginning of 2004, Mohan Bhagwat, an important functionary of the RSS, said that it was now time that the temple agenda was taken up once again in right earnest.

Atal, however, continued till the end of his term; but insiders say that he believed that on the basis of his stellar economic performance that had led to 'India Shining', he would have won. He perceived the Gujarat riots and his failure to rein in Modi as being responsible for the BJP losing the 2004 elections. Nonetheless, looking at Atal's career, it can safely be asserted that for most of his political life he was able to negotiate with the RSS quite ably, failing only during the last period of his tenure as prime minister.

ELEVEN

Revving up the Economy

ACCORDING TO NEWTON'S THIRD law of motion, every action has an equal and opposite reaction. This holds true for the physical sciences, but in the field of policy reforms and political moves, while every action leads to a reaction, the reaction is not equal to the action. In some cases, the reaction is greater than the action and in others it is the reverse. This in a way sums up what happened subsequent to liberalization in the country, though thankfully the reaction was less than the action. Although the clamour for liberalization was building up for many years before 1991, the process, once started, brought in its wake a lot of opposition from a host of quarters. Although the BJP was a supporter of an open economy, there were misgivings within the party too and more specifically within the RSS. Many in BJP circles apprehended that wholesale liberalization would change the industrial landscape in such a way that all domestic players would be thrown out of business. Moreover, consumers would be fleeced in this scenario even as foreign players would dominate business and also create unemployment by large-scale downsizing. Thus there was a need to protect indigenous industry and become industrially self-reliant. The Swadeshi Jagran Manch

(SJM) was set up as an affiliate of the RSS at the end of 1991 to work towards this end. Though the organization was set up with the blessings of Dattopant Thengadi, the senior RSS man who ran the Bharatiya Mazdoor Sangh, it also had the cooperation of Govindacharya, the then general secretary of the BJP and a close Advani associate.

In the Congress raj of Narasimha Rao, the organization had a limited role but once a BJP government came into power, the supporters of the organization had more expectations from it. Immediately, therefore, the SJM stepped up its operations. However, at the same time, the government was being pushed into taking more proactive steps towards liberalization by other interest groups. This was because economic reforms were perceived to be one of the ways of speeding up the growth rate of the economy, something that was desperately needed.

Thus, Atal Bihari Vajpayee faced a dilemma whether to go ahead with liberalization or not. Atal came to a conclusion fairly soon. Liberalization was a one-way street. The rate at which liberalization would be pushed through could be negotiated but the path to be taken was clear. There was no going back or reversal. Not only was this the need of the hour but it was also the need of the country and Atal was firm that the reforms process would go on. In fact, Atal's impulses were liberal from the very beginning.

In 1957, soon after he became an MP for the first time, Atal heard Prime Minister Nehru saying in the Lok Sabha that the government would build hotels. Atal was aghast. He got up and said the government should build hospitals not hotels. Nehru turned around to see who this impudent MP was and retorted, 'We will earn profits from hotels that we will use to build hospitals.' However, Atal remained unconvinced at this blind aping of the policies of communist USSR. From 1999 onwards, when Atal's government was sworn in for the third time, till September 2002, there was rapid liberalization with the blessings of the prime minister himself. Atal's finance minister Yashwant Sinha, is his February 1999 budget, announced the government's intention of privatizing public sector undertakings, not just disinvesting shares.

After 2002, Atal's influence seemed to have waned and he was unable to go any further on the road towards liberalization. Things came to a head with the proposed privatization of two public sector oil companies, Bharat Petroleum and Hindustan Petroleum. These two companies were once multinationals (Esso and Caltex) but had been nationalized in the mid-1970s. They were in the strategic sector and Atal's disinvestment minister Arun Shourie, a gung ho liberalizer, wanted to sell off these two companies. At a cabinet meeting in February 2002, Atal gave the nod in principle for privatizing the two companies. However, as was his style of operating, he left it to the trio of Disinvestment Minister Arun Shourie, Petroleum Minister Ram Naik and Finance Minister Yashwant Sinha to work out the details. That is where the problem arose. Ram Naik, who was close to the RSS bosses, did not believe that it would be right to privatize the oil companies; Shourie thought that Naik was needlessly raising issues because he, as administrative minister of these companies, did not want to lose hold over them, which was bound to happen if they were privatized. Naik, however, had wide support from within the party and also his cabinet colleagues.

NDA Convener and Defence Minister George Fernandes cautioned against the political impact of the move and even IT Minister Pramod Mahajan was apprehensive. Urban Development Minister Ananth Kumar was not sure that the government was proposing to sell at the right price. The final straw came when Deputy Prime Minister L.K. Advani also showed concern about the ministers not being on the same page. Some ministers also expressed the opinion that the two oil companies were nationalized through an act of Parliament; therefore, it was only Parliament which could permit the sale of shares that would make the government a minority stakeholder. A furious debate raged on the issue in the public domain, and reflecting this *India Today* featured a story titled 'Dirty War'. It reported all the differences within the government, and ultimately went on to speculate about a corporate war being played out and ask whether Reliance was the factor that was coming in the way of the sell off. The story pointed out that if Reliance, which was likely to be a bidder, managed to buy even one of the two oil companies, its refining capacity would be equal to that of the government-owned Indian Oil Corporation (IOC). This was because Reliance already owned a refinery and the acquisition of Bharat or Hindustan Petroleum would make it a huge player. If Reliance's capacity equalled that of the IOC, then the Government of India's control over the strategic sector would be challenged. This was the real concern, especially as Reliance in popular perception was seen as an influencer of politics and a player in the corridors of power.

When the matter of the sell off of two oil companies came up again at a cabinet meeting on 7 September 2002, Atal said that he wanted to go forward and hoped that nobody would object. However, ministers started expressing their concern and Ram Naik was unmoved. Atal, a great believer in the power of alliances and consensus knew that it would not be prudent to overrule Naik, not the least because he represented powerful groups which reflected public opinion to a large extent. So the matter was deferred again. Ultimately, the Supreme Court ruled that the acts through which Bharat Petroleum and Hindustan Petroleum were nationalized did not allow for their privatization without prior clearance from Parliament.

Although the privatization of the oil companies was stopped, Atal had always wanted it to happen. In fact, he appointed Arun Shourie, not a career politician, to the job, only because he would not fall prey to political pressures as would any regular neta with various constituencies to cater to. Moreover, Shourie was a tenacious man and would persist with his job without fear or favour. The fact that he had penned books where he had espoused the Hindu point of view meant that he would not be easily targeted by Nagpur.

'Atal appointed Shourie after deeply pondering on the issue. It was no random choice,' says R. Krishnan, then a senior journalist with *Hindustan Times*, covering the economic beat.

Shourie was appointed as minister of the department of disinvestment to begin with; but he would soon run into problems with administrative ministers in charge of companies whose stake were to be sold. To empower him, Atal upgraded the department to a full-fledged ministry. This was also to amply demonstrate the intent of the government.

Atal's determination to privatize was clear soon after he came to power in 1999, when he announced the New Telecom Policy (NTP). Till the policy was announced the government, through the department of telecommunications, was the service provider for telephony. With this new policy, the government vested operation of telephone services in a newly created government-owned company called Bharat Sanchar Nigam Limited (BSNL) in September 2000. The regime for cellular telephony services was also liberalized. This brought more accountability because in the set-up of a government department, there is no transparency regarding the cost of operations and revenues earned.

Videsh Sanchar Nigam Limited (VSNL), a government organization that held the monopoly for long-distance international telephony, was also privatized. This didn't happen without a hitch and raised a huge controversy because VSNL was a hugely profitable company that made ₹800 crore in 2000. Moreover, it had huge cash reserves of more than ₹6,000 crore. The government held 53 per cent of the shares of the company but sold off 25 per cent to the

Tatas and passed on management control to the business house. The company's revenues contributed to the budgetary resources of the government. Analyst Paranjoy Guha Thakurta says that the sale of VSNL alone shows that the Atal government believed ideologically that the state had no role in telephony. Trouble intensified on the VSNL issue when, two months after the sell off, the Tatas used ₹1,200 crore, of the reserves of VSNL to buy into Tata Teleservices Limited (TTL). The knives were out and within the party too Communication Minister Pramod Mahajan got into a conflict with Arun Shourie, the man who had overseen the sale of VSNL. Atal was alarmed but kept his cool and, as was his practice, called Mahajan and Shourie separately and asked them to sort out their differences.

In the period from January 2000 to June 2002, thirteen public sector hotels and twelve other companies were sold off. The companies sold off included Indian Petrochemicals Limited which was hived off to the Reliance group; Maruti, where the government divested its equity to give controlling interest to Suzuki (with whose collaboration the company had been set up); Computer Maintenance Corporation (CMC); Hindustan Teleprinters Limited; Hindustan Zinc; Bharat Aluminum Company (BALCO) and a number of hotels of the India Tourism Development Corporation (ITDC). The Maruti privatization also saw a conflict between Shourie and Ram Naik. Some companies like Jessop in Kolkata (earlier Calcutta), that were earlier private companies that had been nationalized, were also sold off. The first company to be sold off, however, was Modern Food Industries that produced Modern Bread, and it was purchased by Hindustan Lever.

'Companies such as National Aluminum Corporation were also in the privatization list but Atal could not go forward with these companies after the setback in the Bharat Petroleum and Hindustan Petroleum case. Still he has to be applauded for what he delivered, especially considering that he had not been elected to office on the manifesto of privatization,' says journalist R. Krishnan.

Moreover, Atal was leading a coalition government that depended on the support of numerous parties that had different interests and subscribed to different ideologies. Many economists like Columbia University's Arvind Panagariya, who is now the first chief executive officer (CEO) of the NITI Ayog, believe that the high rate of growth in the economy, seen in the first term of the UPA government, was largely a result of the reforms undertaken by the Atal regime. 'In the last fiscal year of Vajpayee's rule 2003–04, growth shifted to over 8 per cent and remained there for a decade,' Panagariya wrote in the *Times of India* on 25 December 2012.

In the same article, he added that Vajpayee propagated reforms proactively and pointed out how addressing the nation from the ramparts of Red Fort, on 15 August 2000, he had said, 'Reforms are the need of the hour; to reform is to turn the inevitability of change in the direction of progress. To reform is to improve the life of every citizen.'

Panagariya also alluded to the fact how reforms, during the tenure of Narasimha Rao, were undertaken a little defensively but under Vajpayee it was different. 'Atal was a liberal man, although some of his ministers like Shourie were right wingers,' says Paranjoy Guha Thakurta.

This enabled Atal to balance out his right-wing ministers. Atal's government began with a growth rate of 6.5 per cent in 1998–99 and, with ups and downs, peaked at a growth rate of 8.5 per cent in 2003–04. Not only this, during Atal's tenure, interest rates were brought down from 14.5 per cent per annum to 9.5 per cent. This was possible because of reduction in the inflation rate. With interest rates down and inflation also reduced, the savings rate also went up from 23 per cent to 30 per cent during this period. A senior official, who was working with the finance ministry during the Atal period (but does not want to be named), says that there was a clear and well-defined strategy. This included emphasis on industrial, agricultural and rural growth, efforts towards revival of exports and development of infrastructure. Efforts were also made to control the fiscal deficit and revenue deficit. 'Atal understood either instinctively or perhaps someone had convinced him, that there was a suppressed demand in the economy and the need was to take various measures to increase production so that this demand could be met. Thus the government took steps to unleash reforms that would allow production to increase by freeing the private sector from unnecessary curbs,' the official says.

But it is for something different that Atal will be remembered till posterity. He kicked off an ambitious programme for highway and road development that connected the four corners of the country. Atal understood that a road network connecting the whole nation would spur economic activity and bring about growth in manifold ways. First, this would give impetus to the highly labour-intensive construction industry when the roads were being laid and would give farmers access to markets once they were ready. Small towns, hitherto in remote and inaccessible areas, would also be brought into the national mainstream if they were connected by roads. Trade would also increase as a result, as the access to ports and urban centres would be used.

'It was a well-conceived programme. And Atalji deserves full marks for implementing the programme that sought to connect the industrial, cultural and agricultural centres of the country,' says Jagdish Shettigar, the then convener of the party's economic cell.

The programme that was called the Golden Quadrilateral programme was ultimately concluded in 2012, with Delhi, Kolkata, Mumbai and Chennai being connected. The network passed through Kanpur, Bhubaneswar, Visakhapatnam, Vijayawada, Bengaluru, Pune, Surat, Ahmedabad and Jaipur to name only a few cities. The programme was financed through a small road cess. Writing in the

Financial Express on 24 December 2014, journalist Sunil Jain points out that while implementing the project, the 'National Highway Authority of India [NHAI] started functioning as a super-efficient private sector firm'.

Atal is also remembered as the man during whose tenure there were reforms in the power sector. While private power-producing companies had been allowed to generate power from the time of the Narasimha Rao regime, the Atal government amended the age-old electricity acts that governed the regulatory framework in the crucial sector. Further, a Central Electricity Regulatory Commission was set up as a quasi-judicial agency. Soon after returning to power in 1999, the Atal government also opened up insurance to the private sector, both domestic and foreign. Interestingly, a similar bill had been introduced by P. Chidambaram during the tenure of the previous government but had been stalled by the BJP, which had then argued that the sector should only be opened to Indian players.

Though Atal was a reformer, he was also a consensus man. This was reflected not only in his reluctance to privatize oil companies once there was opposition to the move, but also in other matters. In the budget of February 2002, Yashwant Sinha had sharply hiked prices of domestic LPG cylinders to cut the huge government subsidy that went to supply cooking gas to consumers. Even though Sinha and his team at the finance ministry were adamant in effecting the price hike, Atal ordered the finance minister to roll back the prices. Insiders say that Atal realized that an anti-middle class budget would harm the image of the government and the party and, therefore, this was not a desirable step. Later in the year, Yashwant Sinha was replaced by Jaswant Singh, who had been the original Atal favourite for the position.

Sinha, a career bureaucrat, had joined the BJP as late as 1993, after serving as finance minister in the Chandrasekhar government in 1991. He was a non-RSS man but had somehow won the confidence of the RSS chief K.S. Sudarshan. This was probably because he had participated vigorously in many RSS Swadeshi programmes. In the party, Sinha was seen as an Advani protégé and, like him, had also been chargesheeted and discharged in the Jain hawala case. However, once Atal appointed Sinha as the finance minister, he continued with him for long and allowed him to present five budgets. Although nobody can doubt the good work done by Sinha, he got into trouble after 2001 with the UTI (Unit Trust of India) scam and some personal allegations against him for favouring his daughter-in-law and another company to whom he had rented his house. These, however, remained mere allegations. More importantly, Sinha had in these years become close to Atal but had lost the confidence of the Swadeshi lobby and Dattopant Thengadi was openly gunning for him. In the end, in July 2002, Sinha was divested of his finance ministry charge and sent to the ministry of external affairs.

TWELVE
Exiting Power

WISE MEN SAY THAT a combination of bad luck and overconfidence can lead anyone to disaster. Ask Atal Bihari Vajpayee. If stories narrated by insiders are correct then, buoyed by the great performance of the Atal government, NDA ally Chandrababu Naidu, then the chief minister of Andhra Pradesh and a powerful voice, began lobbying sometime in late 2003 for early national elections. In the normal course, the elections were slated for October 2004. Realizing that he himself would not be able to convince Atal, Naidu roped in Venkaiah Naidu, who was the president of the BJP and had earlier been the agriculture minister in the Atal government. Venkaiah was game, but the problem was that Atal was not a man who was swayed easily. The duo then took the help of Pramod Mahajan, another minister in the Atal government, who was seen as a mover and shaker in Delhi's corridors of power. Mahajan convinced Atal that under him India was shining and the rising growth rate of the economy was a clear indicator of this. So when the going was good, why not seek the confidence of the public and get another five-year term?

The three also pointed out to Atal that in the assembly

elections in Madhya Pradesh, Rajasthan and Chattisgarh, the BJP had come out with flying colours. The BJP's official site details why early elections were called for in 2004. Among the reasons listed are that the popularity of the prime minister was at an all-time high, the economy was on an upswing and the foreign exchange reserves of the country had crossed the psychological barrier of US$100 billion. Further, India had become a software superpower and a telecom revolution was sweeping across the country. More importantly, even the media was reporting that the elections would lead to the BJP winning comfortably; some sections even asserting that the party could get a two-thirds majority.

At the best of times, Atal was not an instant decision maker and took his time to mull over a problem; but in this case he got convinced about the logic behind the argument and taken in by the hype. So the polls were officially declared and on 6 February 2004, the Lok Sabha was consequently dissolved. However, three weeks earlier, at the national executive meeting of the BJP at Hyderabad on 12 January 2004, an overconfident Atal had announced his decision to go in for early polls in his characteristically poetic way:

> The BJP is not merely a political party but a movement for social transformation. More and more classes of people are joining us. There is a debate on when to hold the polls for Lok Sabha. The party has recommended unambiguously that we should seek the people's mandate at the earliest for completing the unaccomplished part of our mission. We should have a fresh mandate so that we can march more confidently towards our goal of making India a developed nation by 2020. The recent NDA meeting has authorized me to take a final call. Now the responsibility is on me. The NDA is ready, the BJP is ready. The hour of deciding has come. The decision can only be one. I hereby direct

Finance Minister Jaswant Singh to take an early vote on account.

The first fallout of this decision was that Atal's finance minister, Jaswant Singh, was deprived of the chance to present a budget that would have come on 28 February. Since the economy was on a roll, Jaswant could have taken liberties and presented a please-all-budget. After the budget had been cleared by end of April or beginning of May, elections could have been announced. The thinking was that the elections should be held before the onset of monsoons. If the rains were not good, then the wrath of the voter would be unleashed on the ruling party. Atal's men had gambled on a quick election after the announcement, but the Election Commission had its own compulsions; the voters' roll needing to be updated and the like. As a result, the polls could be held only after 20 April, with a gap of seventy-five days. This in turn allowed the main opposition party, the Congress, to get its act together and finalize its alliances and campaigns.

The BJP went to polls all guns blazing with the 'India Shining' campaign. The campaign, as the name suggests, focused on how well India was doing. It neglected bread-and-butter issues, but sought to impress voters by emphasizing economic advancement and rapid growth of the country under Atal's leadership. It talked about the highways being built in the country and other infrastructural developments. The campaign was lopsided because it was focused on the urban growth story and neglected the distress and backwardness in rural India. In line with this, the government failed to use the millions of tons of foodgrains rotting in the godowns of the Food Corporation of India (FCI) even as thousands of farmers and other rural folk, reeling under drought in several parts of the country, were crying for food. At the same time, wheat and sugar and other foodstuffs were being exported from the country.

The slogan 'India Shining' was initially developed as part of the Government of India's campaign to promote India internationally and the nuts and bolts of the campaign were conceived and implemented by the advertising agency Grey Worldwide. A massive ₹150-500 crore was spent on television and print advertisements. Taken in by the campaign, the BJP bosses went to election with this slogan.

A decade later, speaking to *India Today*, Sudhanshu Mittal, a close aide of Pramod Mahajan's, said, 'It was his [Pramod Mahajan's] brainchild. And the idea was to improve the international image of the party. There was a feeling that India was on the move and we were hoping that this campaign would get us more international investment.'

Says Ramesh Chandra, a doctor, 'India Shining meant that there was a feel good factor across the country. But while the upper middle classes were feeling so, it was not true of everybody. It is here that the BJP bosses made a mistake and Atal did not step in and tell them to stop promoting this.'

When the election results came out, Atal and his government had been edged out of power. From 182 in 1999, the BJP's tally had fallen to 138 in 2004. The Congress that had won 114 seats in 1999 had improved to 145 seats. Of course, Atal had himself retained his Lucknow seat by a large majority. That was but natural. He was an icon. Atal polled about 3,00,000 votes and this was 2,00,000 votes more than his nearest rival, Madhu Gupta of the Samajwadi Party. Eminent lawyer Ram Jethmalani was also in the fray. There were twenty-four candidates in all.

The peculiarity of the Indian electoral system is that there is no one-to-one translation of votes into seats. Thus the BJP may have won forty-four seats less in 2004 compared to 1999, but in terms of votes it polled only about 1.5 per cent less votes. In 1999, the party had won about 24 per cent votes and in 2004 it polled

22 per cent. What is more interesting is that the Congress polled a lower percentage of votes in 2004 as compared to 1999. Yet it won more seats. In all fairness, the Congress had polled 28 per cent votes in 1999, nearly 4 per cent more than the vote share of the BJP, yet it had won sixty-eight seats less than the saffron party. Truly, Indian politics is the art of the possible and often like a game of dice where chance plays a big role in throwing up results.

A more substantial reason for the failure of Atal and the BJP to win the 2004 elections was that the saffron party had begun to resemble the Congress. Before it came to power, the BJP used to chide the Congress. Once in power, all the BJP worthies and more interestingly even the cadres began to behave in exactly the same fashion as Congressmen. There was nothing to distinguish the two in the eyes of the public. 'Once in power, the BJP began to look like the Congress. So there was no special reason to vote for the party and Atal Bihari Vajpayee. I voted for the BJP in 1999 and for a change that I think is good for democracy, voted for Congress in 2004,' says Sudhir Dua, a bank officer.

Even in form the Atal government was no different from the government that came before it. Just as an example, when Atal went on overseas journeys, his ministers saw him off at the airport and waited for him when he arrived. Like other PMs before him, Atal was also obsessed with photo ops, although his PR men may have been forcing him into this. This upset many voters who were not emotionally connected with the BJP but just wanted good governance. The instances of corruption that surfaced were shocking for voters who had believed that the BJP was a party with a difference. Bangaru Laxman, the president of the BJP, was caught on tape taking bribe for pushing through a defence deal to buy night vision binoculars in a sting operation by a news magazine. Defence Minister George Fernandes, a close associate of Atal's, was also accused of buying coffins for the martyrs of the Kargil conflict at exorbitant rates, in what was termed as the coffingate scandal.

Apart from ideologically neutral voters like Dua and core Hindu supporters of the BJP, the voters were upset with the performance of the Atal government because the party had done nothing to further its agenda on building a Ram temple at Ayodhya in the five years that it was in power. It had neither abrogated Article 370 that gave special status to Kashmir nor taken any steps to introduce a uniform civil code. The party did not raise the Ram Janmabhoomi issue in the election campaign, disappointing this voter base. Since composite talks were scheduled with Pakistan a few months later, the issue of relations with that country could also not be raised. Political pundits say that creating noise around relations with Pakistan always has the potential of raking in some votes and these votes too were lost to the BJP.

There is a perception that the Bharat Uday Yatra, undertaken by Atal's deputy L.K. Advani, also had the impact of taking away some sheen from the campaign. The yatra involving an 8,500-kilometre drive, covering 121 constituencies in sixteen states in two phases, was undertaken by Advani (in his own words in his autobiography) because: 'Atalji's mobility was restricted by two knee operations in 2002, I had to shoulder responsibility of the campaign.' This in a way contradicted the overall message of the BJP: 'Vote for BJP because of Atal's proven stewardship, the visionary leader who could take India forward on the path of progress and global prestige.'

Says journalist Sanjay Kapoor, 'If votes were being asked in the name of Atal why was Advani going round seeking them? Was this his way of subtly projecting that he was in the running for the leadership? At least in some places, the voters had some doubts. They were wondering if an alternative power centre had been resurrected. This went some way in taking away votes from the party.'

Party President Venkaiah Naidu tried to make light of the

dual power centre theory by terming Atal the 'Vikas Purush' (development man) and Advani the 'Loh Purush' (iron man). By doing so he wanted to give the impression (possibly rightly) that the two complemented each other.

'Brand Atal did not work for other reasons too. Buoyed by success, there was overconfidence that led to many mistakes in political alliances,' says journalist R. Krishnan. A good example is the alliance with the DMK, which the BJP jettisoned for the 2004 election. The DMK tied up with the Congress and delivered all the thirty-nine seats in Tamil Nadu to the UPA and this was a major reason for the party securing a higher tally. In the Atal during tenure from 1999 to 2004, Chandrababu Naidu used to wield great clout. He was the man who sabotaged Atal's initial proposal to elevate Vice President Krishna Kant to the post of president. Instead, he came up with the idea of nuclear scientist A.P.J. Abdul Kalam as the President of India and followed his proposal through. However, in the elections Naidu, who was disconnected from the rural masses, also lost power to the Congress, taking away seats from Atal's kitty. In the 1999 elections, the TDP had contributed thirty-six out of the forty-two seats to the NDA government's tally. But in 2004, this was down to five. Similarly, by dropping the DMK, the NDA did not get a single seat in Tamil Nadu.

The Gujarat riots of 2002 were also responsible for consolidating Muslim and minority votes, that accounted for 15 per cent of the total number of votes, against the BJP. This led to a loss of many seats for the BJP in the elections. In fact, after the elections, Atal lamented that his failure to remove Modi from the post of chief minister of Gujarat had cost the BJP dearly.

Speaking to reporters in Kullu in June 2004, Atal said, 'It is difficult to say what all are the reasons for BJP's defeat in the elections but one impact of the [Gujarat] violence was that we lost the elections.'

When the election results came out, Atal was prompt in submitting his resignation. He sportingly said, 'Dear countrymen, we have given up office but not our responsibility to serve the nation. We have lost an election but not our determination. Victory and defeat are part of life, which have to be viewed with equanimity.'

He especially thanked the people of Jammu & Kashmir for once again reposing faith in democracy and 'for giving a rebuff to the forces of militancy'.

Atal may have taken his defeat with equanimity but the knives were soon out in the Sangh Parivar. Ashok Singhal, president of the VHP said that the NDA had lost power because Atal, along with Advani, had failed to look after the interests of the Hindus.

'Hindus had great expectations from Vajpayee. To their utter surprise, Vajpayee and Advani turned aggressive against the very agitation [Ram Janmabhoomi] that brought them to power.' Singhal added that the party needed a Hindu face, pointing to Madhya Pradesh where the party had come to power with a Hindu face in Uma Bharti.

RSS supremo K.S. Sudarshan was unrelenting. In the an episode of the widely viewed *Walk the Talk* programme with senior journalist Shekhar Gupta, the RSS boss said that Atal should make way for a younger leader. 'I have been saying that he should go and let younger faces emerge. He should stay as senior advisor only. Age is a factor after all.'

Not only this, Sudarshan, who had been kept in check by Atal for a long time, turned nasty by casting aspersions on BJP's performance under Atal. He maintained that Atal had done no remarkable work as PM as compared to his predecessors like Indira Gandhi and P.V. Narasimha Rao. Sudarshan alleged that Atal had found it difficult to check the interference of his son-in-law Ranjan Bhattacharya in government and party affairs. Sudarshan also alleged that Atal's principal secretary and national security advisor, Brajesh Mishra, was hobnobbing with the Congress. Sudarshan said that when he pointed this out to Atal, the latter was annoyed.

Atal, who was over eighty years old at that time, was quite upset with the continual sniping. He had served as prime minister for five years and this was the ultimate that he could aspire for. At the same time, he was plagued by health problems. A close aide of his recollects how even a few years earlier while still the prime minister, he had remarked privately that the silence between sentences in public speeches (for which Atal was well-known) was lengthening because he was not able to connect the ideas so well. Thus, Atal began to mull over whether to call it a day. For starters, he refused to be the leader of the opposition in the newly constituted Lok Sabha. He pushed Advani for the job and promised to share it with him informally. At this time, the press asked him whether he would again become prime minister in the event of the BJP winning the next election. Atal's answer is revealing. 'I do not know what will happen then. Sonia Gandhi is the Congress president, not the prime minister. But this has not affected her work in any way,' he was quoted as saying on Rediff.com on 12 June 2004.

The final announcement of retirement from active politics came at the party's meeting in Mumbai at the end of 2005, at the city's historic Shivaji Park. Atal indicated that he would want the party to now be led by the new Ram–Lakshman jodi of Advani and Pramod Mahajan. Atal was now to become a Bhishma Pitamah, a senior statesman, who would not directly participate in politics but offer advice from the sidelines. This senior statesman role was widely recognized even by his political opponents. In fact, his successor, Congressman Manmohan Singh hailed him as such in 2008. Incidentally, the departure of Atal was also accompanied by the stepping down of Advani from the post of party president. Advani's exit had been imminent for the previous six months. He had made a controversial statement during a visit to Pakistan where he had lauded the founder of Pakistan, Mohammed Ali Jinnah. This had raised hackles in India and even the RSS was not amused. Advani was replaced by Rajnath Singh who had earlier been a minister in Atal's government and was also sometime chief minister of Uttar Pradesh. Pramod Mahajan, who was Atal's chosen man, exited the scene in an unfortunate way in 2006. He was shot by his brother due to a family dispute and died in hospital a few days later.

With the sidelining of Advani and exit of Pramod Mahajan, the ground was fertile for Gen Next to take over the BJP; yet there was no one charismatic enough to take on the mantle. Thus Advani was back as the mascot of the party and led the BJP in the 2009 elections. There was no question of Atal even campaigning for his party candidates; his health had taken a hit at the beginning of the year. In fact, Atal had participated in an electoral campaign for the last time in 2007 end, when Punjab was going to polls. An Akali–BJP alliance led by Prakash Singh Badal was expected to be elected. Speaking at a rally with the skies overcast, Atal quipped in his characteristic manner, '*Badal gadgada rahein hain, mausam badalne waalein hai* [The clouds are thundering; the weather is about to change].'

Atal was hospitalized at New Delhi's AIIMS on 6 February 2009 for chest infection and fever. As his condition deteriorated and he suffered a stroke, Atal had to be put on ventilator. The stroke left him with his speech impaired. The only other time he had a serious ailment (after his back problem during the Emergency) was the trouble that he had while walking due to wobbly knees. This was when he was prime minister and it had started tongues wagging. After a knee replacement surgery at the Breach Candy hospital in Mumbai in 2001, his health had improved.

Unable to campaign in 2009, Atal, however, issued a page-long letter to the electorate of Lucknow, which had elected him to the Lok Sabha five times. He said that the BJP candidate Lalji Tandon had the same qualities as him and thus would prove to be a worthy successor to him. The electorate heeded the call made by Atal and returned Lalji as the winner.

Ultimately, Atal recovered and came back home. But since that day, the former prime minister has been more or less confined to his home on a wheelchair. Once in a while he is taken to the AIIMS for a check-up. The stroke has had a debilitating effect on Atal. Not only has it impaired him physically but also mentally. Beginning with dementia, the man with a golden tongue now suffers from Alzheimer's. Atal is also suffering from the effects of long-term diabetes. He hardly recognizes anybody and eating has become an ordeal for him. For a man who was always surrounded by friends, hardly anyone comes to meet him these days. Among the few visitors that he has is N.M. Ghatate, his friend of six decades, and L.K. Advani. On his birthday, however, many of his admirers throng his house. The last birthday, when the Bharat Ratna was conferred on him, the number of visitors was much larger. Although Atal's visitors are limited, the list of his admirers is large and ever growing. His admirers cut across ages, and even many of the younger generation view Atal with respect and are influenced by his life.

THIRTEEN
A Statesman Par Excellence

'HE WAS A STATESMAN, He was powered by a wider vision,' says N. Chandrababu Naidu, who worked closely with Atal when the latter was prime minister. Naidu echoes the commonly accepted view about Atal among the political class and other citizens.

'His statesmanship transcended politics,' Nobel Prize-winning economist Amartya Sen said after Atal was conferred the Bharat Ratna.

'He was more a statesman than a politician,' Brajesh Mishra told a TV channel many years after Vajpayee had vacated the prime ministerial post.

Prime Minister Narendra Modi tweeted after the Bharat Ratna was awarded to Atal, 'Atalji means so much to everyone. A guide, inspiration and a giant among giants, his contribution to India is invaluable.'

'He was the right shade of saffron. What made him a skilful, experienced and a successful leader was his ability to build consensus,' says journalist Sanjay Kapoor, not particularly fond of the saffron brand of politics.

Atal came to Delhi in 1950, barely twenty-five years old, just as the Indian republic was beginning to be constructed and the country was giving itself a Constitution. Atal was beginning his political innings and the republic was beginning its journey.

'Atal learnt a lot from Delhi as the years progressed and thus became a quintessential part of the Delhi Establishment,' says journalist Saeed Naqvi. Delhi was the political capital and the Parliament where Atal went, allowed a vantage point that gave him a bird's eye view of what was happening across the country. This gave him a sort of detached view and enabled him to rise above the party line. It also made him realize what makes India tick and appreciate the unity in the diversity of the country.

In those early days of the Indian republic, the Congress was the only political outfit of any consequence. The party straddled the political spectrum and its philosophy became the philosophy of the country. Many parties like the Jana Sangh, the socialists, the Swatantra Party and the communists differed from the policies of the Congress. However, such was the grip of the Congress and its leader Jawaharlal Nehru over the country, that they could do precious little.

'All the parties were like planets moving around the omnipresent Congress party that was akin to the sun and it seemed that there would never be a sunset for the Congress party. It was thus remarkable for someone like Atal Bihari Vajpayee to stick on and actually prosper. This is a mark of his statesmanship,' says Amit Chaudhuri who grew up in Delhi during the 1960s, a time when many political parties and numerous opposition politicians rose and fell and disappeared into oblivion without being able to leave any mark.

Atal's potential was recognized by Jana Sangh workers even in the 1960s when the leadership was thrust on him after the sudden demise of Deen Dayal Upadhyaya. Workers, heartbroken at the removal of Deen Dayal from the scene, would raise the slogan, *'Andhera chhatega, sooraj niklega* [The darkness will be dispelled and the sun will rise].' When BJP was formed, with the lotus as its symbol, '*Aur kamal khilega*', was added on to the slogan. These slogans were aimed to highlight Atal's leadership and project the great future that the party had. Incidentally, slogans of, '*Abki baari Atal Bihari*', were raised by the BJP workers from 1995 onwards in the run-up to the 1996 elections. (However, some old timers assert that they have heard this slogan in the late 1960s also.)

It is not the fact of his survival in treacherous Delhi that is the high water mark of Atal's life but his ability to fashion an opposition party that could challenge the ruling Congress party. In other words, he was able to position himself as an alternative and be recognized as one. His potential was realized by none other than Mohammedali Currim Chagla, former chief justice of Bombay High Court and a union cabinet minister. Chagla said, at the first session of the BJP in 1980, 'In BJP, I see an alternative to the Congress and in Atal Bihari Vajpayee, I see an alternative to Indira Gandhi.'

Atal realized that if the Congress party was successful in hanging on to power, it was because it reflected the desires and aspirations of the citizens in some measure. The easiest course for an opposition party is to launch a course of action and espouse an ideology that is diametrically opposed to that of the ruling party. However, Atal never aspired to do so. He knew that if the Congress party was doing something right, it had to be imbibed even at the risk of being criticized.

'Strange that it may seem now, oftentimes we used to say that Jana Sangh was the B-team of the Congress,' says Arun Kumar, a political worker with the Socialist Party in the 1970s.

Incidentally, when Atal became prime minister, his bête noire Balraj Madhok was quoted in *India Today* as saying, 'Vajpayee's prime ministership would be a disaster. He is basically a congressman.'

To say that Atal as the Jana Sangh president, from 1968 onwards, was copying everything that the Congress party was doing would be a travesty of the truth. He was only accepting that part of the Congress belief system that was in sync with the beliefs of the people of the country.

The Jana Sangh had its independent line in most policies where the Congress line began to diverge from ground realities. In Indira Gandhi's heyday, in the early 1970s, Atal began to realize that many of the policy decisions were being taken by the government not because they were in sync with people's desires but because Indira believed they would help her perpetuate her rule. Atal also realized that Indira was trying to damage all democratic institutions for of this reason. This included the legal system, where judges in the highest court were being superseded. Therefore, he began to oppose Indira Gandhi virulently. Things came to a head in the aftermath of the Emergency, with opposition parties coming together to form the Janata Party. The Janata Party broke up in less than three years owing to internal tensions. However, Atal tried hard, bending over backwards, to prevent this from happening. He realized that the era of Congress domination was coming to a close, because people were weary of a single party and a single—Gandhi—family rule. Atal maintained that only a party that combined the strength of the opposition could take on the might of the Congress. That was not to be because the socialists were hell-bent on kicking the ex-Jana Sangh members out of the Janata Party.

Atal was convinced that the way of the Janata Party was the only way forward; so he set up the BJP along the same lines. He felt that the philosophy of the Janata Party, a democratic line that did not discriminate amongst people on caste and creed, was best suited for the country.

But times change and ideologies of a country change with changing generations. In the mid-1980s, with the Indian republic three decades old, the beliefs of earlier times were undergoing change. India was always a Hindu-dominated country with Hindus forming 85 per cent of the population. Though the culture and the mores of the country were Hindu, this was couched in secular terms—*sarva dharma sambhava*. Till then the Congress was a soft Hindu party, its Hinduness masked behind a secular face. Now, in the 1980s, the Congress party was itself revealing an increasingly Hindu face. In view of the fact that the Jana Sangh had been seen as a Hindu party, Atal would have been expected to fashion the BJP with a Hindu face. However, Atal had learnt his history lessons well and resisted the pressure to revert to the Jana Sangh. He knew that in this vast country where millions of people speaking dozens of different languages, thousands of different dialects and professing numerous faiths lived, only a political party that held the middle ground could survive.

His colleagues in the BJP and the Sangh Parivar would not agree. Thus the Ayodhya movement and the mobilization of Hindus began. Atal had the sagacity to realize that this was a movement that could increase the popularity of the party in parts of the country but could never bring it to power in New Delhi. The popularity would at best be short-lived.

As subsequent events show, Atal was prescient. On his own and without being prompted by anyone, Advani, who had led the Ram Janmabhoomi movement, announced in 1995, ahead of the 1996 general elections, that Atal Bihari Vajpayee would be the prime ministerial candidate of the BJP. Advani, whose stock went up with this gesture, realized that the polity was still fragmented. The Congress was collapsing and the BJP was rising, but the strength of the saffron party was not enough to bring it to power. To come to power the BJP, which was treated as a political untouchable by most, would need allies. His calculations proved correct. The BJP came to power under the umbrella of a disparate NDA that only a statesman like Atal could hold together. Atal helped to overcome the untouchability factor.

'Many politicians and political parties did not like the BJP as a party but liked Atal as a person. So they were willing to do business with the BJP, putting their faith in Atal,' confesses a senior BJP leader who does not want to be identified.

The NDA had regional constituents like the TDP, BJD, Akali Dal and JD (U) that had little in common. They had disparate interests but after two false starts in 1996 and 1998, Atal sewed them together. The normal tendency as the leader of alliance would be to ram through the agenda of the dominant partner. Atal took care to distance himself from the core agenda of the BJP and resist attempts made by the RSS and Sangh Parivar outfits to pursue the Hindutva line unrelentingly. This was a mark of his statesmanship. 'Do not forget that Atal's regime was preceded by two short-lived governments. Expectations were at the lowest ebb. Atal was conscious of this,' says an additional secretary to the Government of India who wishes to be remain anonymous.

In fact Atal realized that after coming to power, governance rather than politics would have to be in the driving seat. Speaking at the national executive meeting of the BJP on 15 April 2000, he said, 'What after political success? We are in power at the centre and in several states. We have to concentrate on improving the quality of governance. Governance must concentrate on serving the people and keeping national interests paramount.'

A year later, when Parliament was attacked by terrorists, he realized the import of the matter and how to deal with it. He said, at an emergency national executive committee meeting of the BJP in New Delhi on 29 December 2001 (barely a fortnight after the attack), 'The terrorist attack on Parliament has created a situation that is without precedent. No self-respecting nation that values its freedom can take it lying down. I urge the Party and in fact all political parties to launch a Jan Jagaran [mass awareness] campaign to educate our people about the developing situation.

Our endeavour should be to take along each section of our diverse society with us.'

In fact, this theme of taking everyone together had been a constant feature of Atal's political life. As early as 1982, barely two years after the formation of the BJP and after the bitter experiment of the Janata Party, Atal asserted (at the national council meeting of the BJP at Surat from 4–5 June):

> The greatest curse, not merely of Indian politics but of national life as a whole, is the general incapacity to work together. Let's learnt to unite, instead of dividing to create harmony where disharmony exists and to keep our self-interest and ego in leash. Within the Janata Party not once during those three years of its existence did we witness any serious debate on a principle or public issue. Those regarded as stalwarts of the Janata Party became immersed in power lust.

Atal also alluded to how centre–state relations in the country had become akin to saas–bahu relations.

Atal's realism was seen in his economic policies. Although a product of an era where the public sector controlled the commanding heights of the economy, Atal resisted pressure of going back on the liberalization that was kick-started by the Manmohan Singh government in 1991. There was pressure on him not only from his own Sangh Parivar but also from trade unions and other sundry groups. He realized that India needed accelerated economic growth to eradicate poverty and this could only come through liberal economic policies. It was the turn of the century and Atal recognized that times were changing. The young population was bourgeoning and it had new aspirational dreams. Though he was more than seventy-five years old then, Atal appreciated that status quo could not continue—notwithstanding what most from his generation would say.

'Atal Bihari Vajpayee became the favoured leader of the aspiring classes and in fact was so even in the run up to the elections that brought him to government,' says senior journalist Kumar Ketkar.

Atal's forward-looking economic policies were much appreciated by the private sector but he took care to ensure that he was never seen as being close to private sector barons. Thus, he was industry friendly but not industrialist friendly. This was a great asset and nobody ever brought any charges of favouritism or corruption against him; nobody could accuse him of promoting crony capitalism. At the same time, he was mindful of the social obligations of his government. Therefore, he initiated the Sarva Shiksha Abhiyan that was aimed at universalization of elementary education in a time-bound manner.

'In fact, Atal had realized early in his political career that [first] the Jana Sangh and [later] the BJP would have to be the parties of common men and not those of the rich and the powerful. There were many parties of the rich and the powerful, at least in the Jana Sangh days, and they got considerable votes and more seats than the Jana Sangh. They also professed a liberal economic policy like that of the Jana Sangh but for Atal they were a no-no,' says a BJP leader, preferring not to be named.

'No prime minister can be successful in running a government without taking the bureaucracy along with him. After all, the bureaucracy implements the policies. So their cooperation is of paramount importance. If the bureaucracy does not buy into the policies of the government and is not comfortable with them, they will go to any extent to sabotage them. Atal was somehow able to foster that confidence in the bureaucracy. This, in turn, helped him to run the government smoothly,' the additional secretary quoted earlier says.

Another joint secretary-level IAS officer, who held important posts in the Atal government, says that in the Westminster system of government that India has, the prime minister is the first among equals. 'Atal believed in this and allowed his ministers a huge amount of autonomy. He believed in a democratic fashion of governance. Unless it was really essential, files did not go to his level. The minister in charge of a department took a call on various matters. This gave him acceptability.'

This IAS official also points out that, like many other prime ministers, Atal did not pit bureaucrats against ministers. He also did not have any pet fads, the pursuit of which could have diverted the attention of his ministers and officers. Thus, Atal was able to get the cooperation of both his ministers and the bureaucracy.

Atal was a man who had no dogmas. He responded to the call of the times. Although (as highlighted in the introductory chapter) he had delivered a stirring speech on Tibet in the Lok Sabha in 1959, by the time he became the prime minister, he realized that much water had passed through the Tsang Po and Brahmaputra. Thus in June 2003, Atal formally recognized Tibet as part of China, which de facto it was. The idea was to take a positive step forward to solve the problems with China that had been festering since 1962. He also believed that 'you can change friends but not your neighbours', and that is why he aggressively pursued peace with neighbours like Pakistan. In fact, this became an article of faith for the foreign ministry after Atal first propounded this dictum as external affairs minister in the Janata government. Old timers still remember how, in November 2000, Atal declared a unilateral cease fire against Islamic militants in Kashmir in a prelude to peace talks. This cease fire was extended and Pervez Musharraf was invited to talks. Atal took such measures in the face of tough opposition even by a section of his party men. They argued that Pakistan could not be trusted because of its track record of starting the Kargil war just after the Lahore declaration a year earlier. However, Atal was unconvinced by these arguments.

Journalist and author Mayank Chayya, writing in the *Indian Express* (24 December 2014), described Atal as one of the 'finest practitioners of India's enlightened pluralism as embedded in its ancient civilization rather than as mandated by the Constitution of a young nation state'. Chayya recollected that within three days of the Babri Masjid demolition, he said self-assuredly that the whole episode was the BJP's worst miscalculation. In a similar vein, journalist Harish Khare wrote in *Open* magazine (19 December 2014), 'Atal understood how difficult it was to maintain, leave alone impose, any kind of order on this complex and complicated land and that wisdom demanded an approach of accommodation and reconciliation.' He added that Atal 'understood that as PM he had to try and win the confidence and respect of all sections of society. As a ruler of a country that had gained statehood after centuries of internal discord and disunity he was mindful of the painful incomplete journey of nationhood'.

Vinay Sahasrabuddhe, director general of the Rambhau Mhalgi Prabodhini, an organization that is now collating speeches and other materials relating to Atal, writing in *DNA*, said that Atal exuded a 'Main hoon na' image to the general public. The public felt reassured by his presence and confident that he would try his best to ensure that everybody's interest was properly taken care of.

He added, 'All his life he strived to make politics more value-oriented. He contributed to the Indian polity in multiple ways, he is the epitome of alternate political thought and functionality. He has an inimitable style of winning friends. He has several friends with views diametrically opposite to his but this has never come between him and them.'

Indirectly indicating what his beliefs were, Atal had once pointed out in the course of a Lok Sabha debate that the Indian Constitution does not mention the word secularism. Atal said that the members of the Constituent Assembly had discussed what secularism was and come up with multiple views. But during the Emergency (when opposition leaders were in jail), the government had amended the Constitution to declare India, which was till then a democratic republic, a secular socialist democratic republic. Atal said that even when this change was incorporated, Congress MPs had said that Indian secularism is different from western secularism. 'I agree with this, we do not stone anybody to death; we do not put any one on [the] cross.'

He said that India was not a religious state and could never become one. These beliefs were its 'jeevandhara' (essence of life) and were rooted in its soil. Atal added that India was not born a few decades ago in 1947, but was a 5,000-year-old civilization.

Kumara Guru of the Indian School of Business in Mohali, who was still a student when Atal was prime minister, says, 'He was Teflon coated and evoked great confidence in people. They reposed faith in him. No charge against him ever stuck. In fact nobody would even think of charging him of [sic] anything negative. This is the hallmark of a great individual. I think he was greatly underrated as a reformer.'

Senior government officials, who have worked with Atal, say that though he delegated work to other ministers, there was never any doubt that he was in charge. The final call in every complicated matter was taken by him, whether it was related to External Affairs or Internal Affairs. 'He was the boss without giving the appearance of being one, but there was no doubt that he was the boss. His was the last word,' says a joint secretary during Atal's regime.

'I think he was a thorough gentleman and did not intimidate others. The way he conducted himself was statesman-like,' says Seeta Murty, the principal of a school in Hyderabad. 'It is not that there were great expectations of Mr Vajpayee when he came to power. But quietly and without making any big show he was able to deliver a lot. We really saw good governance under him,' she adds.

'He had a quiet confidence, was not a showoff and was easily accessible. People could easily identify with him and also approach him. This was his real strength and these sterling qualities made him the statesman that he was,' says Delhi-based Supreme Court lawyer, Diljit Ahluwalia.

'He was certainly accommodative and diplomatic. The nature of his government demanded that. But in spite of his circumstances he was able to achieve much. To me he comes across as the most underrated PM of India,' says Rajeev Saxena, a bank manager in Delhi.

'His appeal cut across people of different ages, sexes and regions. If the old woman in Kolkata was his fan, so was the young techie in Bangalore. The same could be said about the acceptability of Atal amongst a crowd of executives in Mumbai and a group of farmers in UP,' says Manoj Pant from Lucknow.

'He can be called eclectic akin to ancient philosophers who selected doctrines from various schools of thought. Thus he had imbibed and projected a catholicity of views,' says Supriyo Banerjee, an academic from Kolkata.

'A deep thinking man not given to hasty decisions is what Mr Vajpayee was. None of his steps were impulsive. He had wisdom,' says Sanjay Gadhalay, a product of IIT Kharagpur.

'He was a *pakka* realist. He had been in politics for so many years and gone through so many ups and downs. So he never craved for power and he had grown above this. Nothing really seemed to bother him,' says Kumar Ketkar.

Atal had many achievements, other than those mentioned before, to his credit. Within a year of his coming to power for five years, Atal divided three big states of Bihar, Madhya Pradesh and Uttar Pradesh, creating Jharkhand, Chattisgarh and Uttarakhand. Atal believed in the dictum of small is beautiful and this was in sharp contrast to the Congress line then. The Congress idea was to keep India as it was, possibly because the party bosses realized that breaking India into smaller states could lead to emergence of regional forces that would have their own aspirations. This would challenge the old Congress hegemony over power. Atal realized that in a smaller state the government would be closer to the people and, therefore, he went about the bifurcation of the states. Being the head of a government that had over two dozen constituents, this was not an easy task. However, Atal went ahead in a statesman-like manner only as far as the politics of the day would allow. For this reason, he did not divide Andhra Pradesh to create the state of Telangana and refrained similarly from bifurcating Maharashtra to create Vidarbha. NDA partners like the Telugu Desam Party were virulently opposed to the division of Andhra Pradesh and Atal knew the limitations.

Atal continued the Look East policy in foreign affairs that was started by Narasimha Rao. Atal realized that India had a huge historical connect with South-east Asian countries from ancient times. However, because India had been part of the British Empire, this connect had been lost and India was more focused on relations with the UK, the US, Europe and the USSR. Although these countries were important, it was also necessary to engage with South-east Asian countries that also had a large Indian diaspora besides being part of the same extended civilization. India became part of the BIMSTEC formation that tied Bangladesh, India, Myanmar, Sri Lanka and Thailand. Atal also focused on rebuilding relations with Central Asian republics, with whom India had traditional historical links.

A strong India was an article of faith for Atal. He believed that only a strong India could stand up to enemies and would be respected by other countries. That is the reason why, after nuclear testing, Atal wisely concentrated on upgrading the defence capabilities of the country. Agni-I, a ballistic missile capable of firing nuclear war heads up to a range of 800 km, was tested during Atal's regime. This was followed by the induction of Agni-II that had 2000-km range. Brahmos, the supersonic cruise missile that was a joint venture between India and Russia, was also successfully test fired during Atal's regime.

Atal was described as 'The Smiling Buddha' by *India Today* in its 12 January 2004 issue while declaring him as its Man of the Year for 2003. The cover story by S. Prasannarajan described Atal as the 'Oriental face of reason and resolution, of peace and restraint. Vajpayee is the eldest statesman of the East.' The story also noted that Atal 'handles power with a kind of sagely detachment. He uses renunciation as a means of reaffirmation'. Further Atal was described as 'larger than the political size of his party. He is in it and above it, keeping his moral system beyond the grasp of real politik even beyond the demands of his own party. He has changed the grammar of leadership. His wisdom does not claim copyright over mass conscience. He is the balmy benefactor'. It was quite clear that his long experience of public affairs had made Atal a wise old man; only this accounts for the profuse praise heaped on him by *India Today*.

In the run up to the last elections of his life in 2004, Atal said that he never nursed any ambition to become prime minister. All he wanted was to become a journalist. He also said that he wanted to be remembered as a man who wanted to do 'good' for his country and the world. Atal was also much concerned about the loss of trust in politicians amongst people. However, he held that the politicians were squarely to blame for this.

All through his life, Atal was berated by critics who claimed that he changed his position to suit convenience. Atal, however, knew that the perceived shifts in his ideology had little to do with convenience and were more because of the duality that exists in life. He admitted in a mock trial in the *Aap ki Adalat* programme of

Rajat Sharma that in his belief system, both *Satyartha Prakash* and Karl Marx could coexist and so could Churchill and Chamberlain. Incidentally, *Satyartha Prakash* (literally the light of truth) is an 1875 book written by Swami Dayanand Saraswati, which is the cornerstone of the philosophy of the Arya Samaj that is based on the concept of 'Back to the Vedas'. Dayanand Saraswati believed that ills had entered Hinduism in the later centuries. Whereas Neville Chamberlain, the British prime minister at the beginning of World War II, was known to be practical and willing to compromise, Winston Churchill was seen as a tough nut who was inflexible and unbending.

Those familiar with the game of football or hockey (which, interestingly, is listed on the BJP's website as Atal's favourite game), are aware of the importance of players in the position of halves. They are the linkmen who take the ball from the defenders and pass it on to the forwards who launch a raid on the goal of the opposing team. In some senses, the linkmen hold the team together by playing the role of defenders (stopping the ball before it can go into the goal region) and offenders (sending the ball towards the enemy goal).

If the history of the Indian republic over its sixty-five years of existence, can be likened to a football or hockey match, then Atal roughly played in the position of linkman. He was the man who linked the now-past Nehruvian era to the now-upon-us Modi era. He was the link between the first republic that was and the second republic that is in the works. Without someone like him straddling the two eras, the Indian republic would not be what it is now. This in a way is the ultimate tribute to Atal Bihari Vajpayee, the true mark of his statesmanship.

www.ingramcontent.com/pod-product-compliance
Lightning Source LLC
Chambersburg PA
CBHW030411100426
42812CB00028B/2914/J